In the Face of Presumptions

Barry Moser, Self-portrait at fifty-nine

First published in 2000 by
DAVID R. GODINE, *Publisher*
Post Office Box 450
Jaffrey, New Hampshire 03452
www.godine.com

Library of Congress Cataloging-in-Publication Data
Moser, Barry.
In the face of presumptions : essays, speeches, & incidental writings/
by Barry Moser ; introduction by Paul Mariani ;
edited by Jessica Renaud. — 1st edition.
p. cm.
ISBN: 1–56792–126–4   (hc : alk. paper)
1. Moser, Barry. 2. Illustrators—United States—Biography.
I. Renaud, Jessica. II Title.
NC975.5M68 A2   2000
741.6´092—dc21

First Edition
Printed in the United States of America

In the Face of Presumption

ESSAYS, SPEECHES & INCIDENTAL WRITIN

BY BARRY MOSER

INTRODUCTION BY PAUL MARIANI

EDITED BY JESSICA RENAUD

DAVID R. GODINE, PUBLISHER ❖ BOSTO

FOR M

✤

Nil non mortale tenemus,

pectoris exceptis ingeniique bonis.

— B.M.

FOR M

✧

Nil non mortale tenemus,

pectoris exceptis ingeniique bonis.

— B.M.

CONTENTS

PREFACE

T HE FIRST TIME I met Barry Moser was in 1976. This was at his studio
over on Clark Avenue in Northampton. There was a printing press in the
room behind the counter, and I walked through the door that day with
trepidation and a sheaf of poems called *Timing Devices* and asked Moser—
he had to be called out from whatever task he was busy at—if he would look
them over. The artist, Jack Coughlin—a neighbor of mine—had told me
Moser might—just might—be willing to do a book of poems if he liked them
enough and, knowing absolutely nothing about the publishing business, I
simply asked Moser that day if he thought he might have the time to look
my poems over. My mentor and friend, Allen Mandelbaum, had suggested
the idea, and had promised to pay the expenses of having it printed in a limited edition with some of the money he'd earned for his translation of *The
Aeneid*. That was the kind of man he was. Allen had come up from New York
and I'd driven him over to Northampton to meet Leonard Baskin in his
studio, sitting there among the massive shelves of his towering incunabula,

while the two men talked about Baskin's illustrating the cover for Allen's *Aeneid*.

Baskin was Baskin, unapproachable, arch, brooding, his brilliant eyes seeming to dart and smolder. As soon as I'd walked into his studio, I knew I was out of my element. I was thirty-six, a young professor of poetry, with two inconsequential university press books to my name, a man of no name. Baskin, I remember, distinctly disliked the anti-Semitic Eliot, so much, in fact, that he had recently created a dark, unappealing portrait of the poet for the cover of *The Massachusetts Review*. But Allen refused to allow Eliot to be so summarily dismissed, countering by quoting from memory the lines that open the fifth movement of Eliot's "East Coker," lines that begin this way:

So here I am, in the middle way, having had twenty years—twenty years largely wasted, the years of *l'entre deux guerres*—trying to learn to use words, and every attempt is a wholly new start, and a different kind of failure....

My heart still thrills to those words spoken then by that man, for they might stand as epitaph for what we have all tried to do with the art with problematic resources and the best intentions, Barry Moser included.

Then, I remember, Baskin turned to ask me a question, as much as to say, *I have no time for small talk. And just what are you doing in my house?* I stammered what reply I could. I knew then that I was in the house of some Plutonian god and surely in over my head. I remember praying for deliverance.

The initial meeting with Moser started out in pretty much the same way. Though Barry is six months younger than me, I felt as if I had just met Moses that winter afternoon. Moser is a head shorter than me, but he's barrelchested and powerful, a kind of ruined linebacker, and the sort of ally you want on your side if a fight breaks out in a bar, say. As usual, Moser was in the midst of a bread-making project that day, and Harold McGrath, dear Harold, one of the finest printers this country has produced, was busy in the back room at one of the presses, and so Barry simply looked at me, telling me to leave the poems with him and that he would get back to me with an answer within the month. I did not leave with much hope.

And when, after the month had elapsed, I had heard nothing, I naturally took the silence for a no. Finally, I called to tell him I would come by and pick up the poems at his convenience. I thanked him for his time. He'd yet to read the poems, he told me, but he promised to take them over to Williston Academy, where he was teaching art, read them, and get back to me with an answer the following day. The next day, as good as his word, he phoned me. Waiting for class to begin, he'd pulled a few poems out of the packet and had read them, and something in one of them had goddamn almost made him cry. Hell, he told me, if a poem could do that to him, he was going to go ahead and publish them all. And he did—the result being the most beautiful book of mine ever to see the smoky light of day. Tall, thin, white gray on darker gray, with deckle-edged pages, with five prints scattered throughout, followed by a foldout of all five prints in the back of the book. And these were images dear to my heart, images which we both mulled over, over dinner sometimes, or—as often as not—over good, mellow whiskey. Angels—the recording angels of history, one the alpha, the other the omega, two presences bracketing the junk heap of history, littered with the trucks and jeeps and oil cans of my father's mechanic's world, the dark woods, the three-headed dog that guards the entrance to hell, the graves of the dead. But also the chalice of Antioch, the grapes, the crown of thorns, the cup itself—half Christian, half pagan—recovered from a well or other inglorious dig: the stuff of life transubstantiated by the imagination. A year later, the book was published in a handsome—and affordable—trade edition by David Godine, the same force behind the book of essays you are now reading.

Barry Moser graced my book as he has graced my life, graced other books of mine, though none so grandly as that first, and through the subsequent ups and downs of the past quarter century we have remained good friends. He is one of the handful of people I can say have made a qualitative difference in my life, so much so that I wonder what my life would have been like without him, and I have come to love him as a brother.

Nel mezzo del cammin di nostra vita. Moser and I were both just past the midway point of our allotted seventy years when we first met, and soon, incredibly, we will both turn sixty. In the years I have known him, I have watched him as he undertook larger and larger projects. Yes, the wonderful children's books, beginning with *Jump!*, the retelling—serendipitously—of the old Br'er Rabbit story, a story of survival in the South so dear to Moser.

But also Allen Mandelbaum's long labor of love, his translation of Dante's *Comedy*, and *Moby-Dick*, and *Frankenstein*, and *Jekyll and Hyde*, and the *Alice in Wonderland*, and *The Wizard of Oz*, and—finally—the culminating dream of a lifetime—the illustration and design of the King James Bible, all of it, from Genesis to Revelation, a project which I know has changed his life, as it has mine as I have gone the journey with him, in ways perhaps too deep for words.

Again and again he has astonished me with the work that has appeared from the inspired multiplicity of his etched lines and meticulous brush-strokes. The man has been indefatigable, and when he tells us that he has often worked twelve and fourteen hour days day in and day out on some project, often rising at four or five o'clock to begin work, he is not exaggerating. It is his metier to work, and he has worked and worked and worked, damaging his wrist and forearm with repetitive motion, and losing much of his hearing from the constant whine of his high-speed drills. He has poured himself out in his work in a perfect kenotic emptying of the self, discarding work that you and I, friend, would despair of ever imitating. By now his images—portraits and animals and objects brilliantly and shimmeringly rendered in a variety of media—have marked him as one of our great national treasures.

And then there is his writing, which I have watched grow in suppleness and force and with the grace of some sandal-shod great gray dray horse, if you will, over the past thirty years and more until he has honed for himself a style uniquely his. How rare this is, to find an artist who can work in two such disparate mediums—the image and the word. And for a man who prides himself on a kind of classic narrative linearity, there is surely a multi-dimensionality to Moser's language.

First and foremost, there's the arithmetical discipline of the essays themselves, a calculated sense of form that undergirds all his work. If, then, a spoon (even a silver spoon) appears in the opening paragraph, you can be sure that spoon is going to appear elsewhere in the piece, like a fine leitmotif. There is balance everywhere in Moser's work, whether it be an etching or an essay. Even if the design seems at times to take the elliptical orbit of some comet, you know that Moser's designs are going to turn back on themselves the way a good poem or a good story returns on itself, bringing with it an unexpected intensity of light. His prose can dance, the way the best Southern writing dances, whether it is William Faulkner or Flannery O'Connor or Eudora Welty or Bobbie Ann Mason. How delightful to move continually between the raw, down home speech of Moser's Tennessee forebears, whom he honors so generously here in his own cadences, and the precision of the artist talking about his craft—paper, font, quality of wood, quality of line, page design—and then, as quickly, lifting us to new heights with his periodic riffs. He is someone, this man, who knows by heart the night sounds of the dogs sleeping at his feet as well as he knows good southern bourbon or a good risotto cooked with leeks, onions and butter. But he is a man too who has known the strange otherworldly music of the ineffable calling to him, and wept openly—as I myself have seen him do, bless him—over his long wrestling with (let me say it for him)—the Spirit who has proffered him such gifts.

Here are some twenty-odd pieces, culled over the years, which journal Moser's career, but also open unexpected doors into his own past—his Tennessee boyhood, his years at a military academy in Chattanooga, the Baylor School, mixed in with his fondness for Vernita, his black neighbor, and his own fear of the local Ku Klux Klan, which numbered members of his own family among them. His marriage, his move north to western Massachusetts, his apprenticeship, the growth of a mind, the prodigious reading in the classics as in his contemporaries, the travail of creating each of his major books. I thought I knew this man, but there were revelations on nearly every page for me as well, and I could not put down these essays once I had begun reading them, in spite of all sorts of obligations screaming to be heard. What worked for me may, friend, work for you. The man is contagious, funny, serious, and a needed balm to the soul.

— PAUL MARIANI
December 1999

Portrait of the Artist's Mother

SILVER SPOONS

An Introduction

MY MOTHER ALWAYS TOLD ME that I was born with a silver spoon in my mouth. As a child, those words conjured strange images to mind, but as I grew, I realized it was a figure of speech, something people said but never explained. Still, it is only now, well into the latter half of my life, that I finally understand what she really meant. You see, my Mother believed that I'd always have the capacity—and the good fortune—to live a happy and fulfilled life. And she was right.

I have never had to face any personal trauma or tragedy other than the natural and expected losses of parents, grandparents, aunts, uncles, and beloved pets. I've lost only one close friend.

I have had no crises that have driven me to distraction. There has been nothing so difficult that I haven't been able to cope. Nothing has prevented my living in the world as any ordinary man.

I have been particularly fortunate in that I've never been avaricious at heart. Mother used to say "Why, honey, that nickel's just a-burning a hole in your pocket, isn't it?" because I could not—or would not—save my money. Still don't. I spent money when I had it. Still do. I'm content with what I have.

And because of these great good fortunes I have never been forced to take solace in my work. It has never been a hiding place from afflictions. By the same token, I have never been kept from my work by troubles. No adversity has ever stanched the flow of my work.

All these things have allowed me to maintain a more or less carefree mental stability and an eternally youthful sense of play. Indeed, my work is my life and my joy. I've been willing to dedicate myself to it, and I was smart enough to know that a teaching career—while not known for its wages—would allow me time to pursue my muse, to commit myself to my art and craft.

And therein lies a secret.

I am, as I write this, in the final corrugations of my work on The Holy Bible. If it were not for that innate sense of play, unwavering dedication, unfettered time to do the work, and complete freedom from fiscal constraints that the project itself provided, it would never have been done. These are all my silver spoons. So Mother was wrong. I was born with several silver spoons in my mouth, not just one.

Historically speaking, the Pennyroyal Caxton Bible began in 1985—about the time I was working on *Adventures of Huckleberry Finn*. There was an exhibit of the illustrations I had done for Truman Capote's *I Remember Grandpa* in a small upstairs gallery at the Gotham Book Mart in Manhattan. Early in the evening I was introduced to Mr. Bruce Kovner and his wife Sarah. Kovner was, as I found out, a collector of my books and a serious bibliophile (his Manhattan-based investment management company is the Caxton Corporation, named for the famous English printer of the 15th century). During our conversation that warm New York evening he asked me if there was something that I wanted to do that I had not yet done.

I said, "Yes, I want to do a Bible some day."

"Well, why don't you do it?" he responded.

I said, "To do it the way I want would cost more money than I'm ever likely to have … and besides, I'm not old enough yet." Though I didn't say so at that moment there were two other reasons as well: at the time good engraving blocks were becoming increasingly scarce; and Harold McGrath, my tireless and peerless printer, was going to retire soon. But most of all I knew down deep that I was just not ready. I was not old enough, not experienced enough, certainly not wise enough. Kovner listened and then suggested that if I ever did decide to try my hand at doing a Bible, I should keep him in mind because he might be interested in backing it.

Ten years later I was reminded of that brief conversation by our mutual friend, Jeff Dwyer, and wrote to Kovner. I explained that I felt that the time was now or never if I were going to undertake the first fully illustrated English Bible of the twentieth century. Time would be running out before too long. A few days later, at nine-thirty in the evening, Thursday August 11, 1995, Kovner phoned. He wanted to ask me some questions, hear me describe the project as I envisioned it, and have me run some preliminary financial numbers by him. I tried to stay dignified and composed and answer his questions without stumbling over my own excitement. I got particularly nervous trying to project how much money I thought the project would cost (as it turned out I was off by a mere seventy-five percent). He ended our conversation by saying that "in principle" he would agree to be the "bank" for the project. I went back to my bed and my book feeling dazed and euphoric. I knew that if Kovner were to fund the project it would pave the way for me to realize a longstanding dream.* But I was cautious not to get my hopes up too far. Not just yet.

A week later Kovner called back, saying he had definitely decided to fund the project. I don't remember the rest of the conversation. I had heard what I wanted to hear, and it eclipsed everything else. My dream might just come true after all. The only things that now remained in question were the mechanics of getting it done and my own gumption and energy in seeing that it did. Had I been a religious man, as I once had been, I would have run to the top of my hill and shouted at the top of my voice, Praise God! But, alas I was not a believer—at least not in such a way that would prompt such an ostentatious display—so I busied myself with mindless work, letting my mind glide freely wherever it wanted, feeling humbly grateful to whatever powers and forces brought me to that day.

As I cleaned out drawers and ran the vacuum cleaner that day, it became clear to me that everything I had ever done in my life led me inexorably to this time, this place, and this project. Military school and its emphasis on discipline and drilling, which I am sure has something profound to do with my affinity for type and pages. My religious experiences as a young man— especially the fundamentalism I embraced so that I could later move beyond it. Taking Greek at the University of Chattanooga, though I dropped it during the first semester because I was sure that I wouldn't pass. Studying with George Cress who taught me to paint without subject matter and wield large bristle brushes. Meeting and marrying a woman, Kay Richmond, who was later willing to relocate and live in New England, a place neither of us had even visited. Being introduced to Leonard Baskin who pushed me to draw better than I already could. Meeting Harold McGrath and seeing fine books for the first time at the old Gehenna Press on Clark Avenue in Northampton. John Boynton's bringing me to Bonnie Verberg's attention and her commissioning me to do my first children's book in 1985, which taught how to tell stories with pictures. And Maria Modugno's commissioning me to retell Hans Christian Andersen's *The Tinderbox*, which taught me not only how to write better than I already did but, more importantly, taught me the connection and similarities between the structure of prose and the structure of pictures. And I could go on. But for now it is enough to say that on that hot August day, I felt sure that all these paths, among all the other mews and avenues of my life, paved and unpaved, had led me to the Pennyroyal Caxton Bible.

From where I am now, I see that it took guts—guts to even think about doing a fully illustrated Bible. And it took stamina. And ability. And training. And discipline. And determination. And tenacity. And being willing to fall flat on my face in the feculence of failure and get up, wipe off the mire, and get on with it again. These are the attributes of my abilities. But even all that wasn't enough to do this project. It took something else, and I wish I could plunk down just the right word right here, but I can't. I don't know what it is. It's a mystery. Something compelled me to muster the courage and discipline and stamina, obliged me to marshal the ability, the training, and the tenacity. Something fueled all this so that over four years it never once waned—something other than food, love, encouragement, self-confidence, or gin. And who knows where that comes from? It's a gift, I suppose. And, as prosaic as it may sound, I hope that I have now—in some small way— given that gift away because that's what gifts are really for—to be given, not kept.

What follows is a collection of speeches, essays, forewords, afterwords, and a few lengthy notes that speak to these things. The constant is that each one is a sort of paving stone, part of the macadam that makes up the whole of those avenues that led me to this point in my life, led me to my life's work, led me to this Bible. They speak to the commonplace character of my daily habits and to the hymnody of my work. They speak to the warp and weft of the fabric of life, family, and work—three threads that for me cannot be unspun or unwoven. They speak to my mother's silver spoons.

---

* In March of 1977, the Leverett Craftsmen Center in Leverett Massachusetts invited Fritz Eichenberg, David Bourbeau, Charles Mikolaycak, and me to be on a panel discussing illustration and the book arts. After our presentation questions were taken. One question, addressed to us all, was, "Gentlemen, if you could do any book in the world, what would it be?" Fritz and I answered first and in immediate unison: "The Bible." For me it was not a new thought that evening in Leverett. I had dreamed of doing a fine press edition for seven years—ever since I first learned how to set type and print books in 1969. It became a more powerful dream in 1970 when I saw a copy of the mighty Bruce Rogers lectern Bible in Arno Werner's workshop in Pittsfield, Massachusetts. For years I thought it was decorated and had color running through it. A number of years later, in the cathedral at Ripon, England, I saw one again and realized that it in fact has neither decoration nor color—such is the power of its design.

BACKYARDS, BIRDHOUSES & TOY WARS

For Robert Howell Cox

M Y UNCLE BOB died in 1955. I was fourteen going on fifteen. My brother and I helped the medics lift him onto the gurney and rode in the ambulance with him to the hospital where they told us he was dead. We buried him three or four days later. Even though it was summer, I wore my wool Baylor uniform. Bob was proud that my brother and I went to military school, and my aunt Velma said we should wear it for his sake. His pride, like the rest of the family's, stemmed more from knowing that we boys socialized with the sons of the wealthy and powerful than from knowing we were exposed to a privileged education.

The Baylor uniform, like West Point's and the Citadel's, consisted of gray trousers and tunics with black stripes and chevrons, decorated with colorful patches and braids, and accessorized with Sam Brown belts and brass cross-arms and pips. That uniform was a symbol of a social station my mother once flirted with and the rest of the family envied. I think it was for that reason that our aunt Velma insisted that I wear it to the funeral, never mind that it was summer and we were not supposed to wear our uniforms during vacations.

We buried Bob on that hot, sunny day, but part of him didn't die. Part of him lives on because I speak of him here, and lives on because he was my first real teacher and is subsequently a part of everything I make. He was a craftsman. He made things, all sorts of things: bric-a-bracs for Velma; gun racks which hung in our houses and cradled the hallowed symbols of our collective manhood; plaster-of-Paris candlesticks which every Christmas stood like white sentries beside the front door for the family get-together. He made so many birdhouses that it prompted my cousin Wayland to say that Bob would never die because he had made so many of them. I suppose the ubiquity of those birdhouses suggested to Wayland that Bob had insured his own immortality with the work of his hands.

I was the baby of the family and was used to the slim pickin's and hand-me-downs of that circumstance, especially when it came to clothing and chores. I helped Mother in the kitchen, cooking and cleaning up. I hung out the wash with her and helped fold it and put it away when it was dry. And I was the one who walked down to the corner store to fetch milk or bread because I did it without complaint or sass—most of the time. My older brother, Tommy, did the more masculine chores: mowing the grass, washing the car, trimming the hedges, and cleaning out the gutters.

I didn't mind the indoor chores. In fact, I liked being indoors with my mother and the black woman who came on Mondays to iron for us. Her name was Mattie, and she dipped snuff and rarely spoke, but her presence was comforting and I liked her face. The warmth of this memory had a lasting effect—I named my youngest daughter Madeline. We call her Maddy.

And besides, it was indoors in the winter and on the back porch in the summer where I drew my cowboys and Indians, Royal Canadian Mounted Police, Roman gladiators, monsters & gargoyles, aerial battles, and "nekkid" women. And it was indoors on the back porch where I built model ships and tanks and airplanes out of kits which we could rarely afford to buy, or out of wooden strawberry cartons and tinfoil and cellophane from Velma's cigarette packs and whatever else I could find.

It would probably not be true to say that Bob was the first to notice my penchant for making things, but he was certainly the first one to teach me how to make things better than I already could. In fact, his interest sometimes made my young life miserable because he was gruff and critical.

He'd say "What the hell's a-matter with you boy ... cain't you see that thing ain't square?"

Or, impatiently, "You don't paint across the grain, boy, you paint with the grain."

Or, most commonly, he'd say, "Jesus H. Christ, son, that is the most half-assed goddamn thing I ever saw."

Bob cussed a lot, but his interest, encouragement, and criticism were important to me, even if it did sting and bring tears to my eyes.

My stepfather (the man I always called, and still call, my daddy), on the other hand, told me more than once that it was stupid of me to think that I could pursue a career in art. His boss's son, Charlie Thompson, Jr., had tried to become a commercial artist but ended up selling life insurance, and, Daddy said, if Charlie Thompson Jr. couldn't do it, neither could I. He told me I could never make a living at it. Even after I had a degree in painting and was teaching school, he showed more interest in the football team I coached than he did in the paintings I painted.

I don't remember what my mother thought, though I know that she was always interested in what I learned in school—especially biology—and she encouraged me to continue my education. I think she regretted the slimness of her own and took vicarious pleasure in mine. We talked a lot, cleaning up after dinner. But if she had an opinion about my pursuing a career in art, I don't remember her expressing it. I know she was dead set against my applying to either the Rhode Island School of Design or the University of Cincinnati because they were too far North. She didn't want me to go to school with Yankees. She wanted her baby to stay closer to home. So I ended up at Auburn University in Alabama as an Industrial Design major, then, later, at the University of Chattanooga as a painting major. Mother died before I did any mature work.

My brother took no interest at all. After we got to be a certain age—eight or nine—he either ignored me, beat me up, or ridiculed me.

Uncle Bob, on the other hand, made my first drawing table for me and for that I will love him forever. That gesture was my first real endorsement—all the more important because it came from him who always criticized me for being half-assed. He made it out of a discarded bedside table he had salvaged from some hospital or clinic in the territory he covered as a surgical supply salesman. I used it for years, but it got broken in the move from Tennessee to New England and I, like a damned fool, threw it away rather than fixing it as Bob would have done.

I venerate Bob, though if he were alive today, we would probably be as estranged as I am from what little of my family is still left. As likely as not, he too would disapprove of my life-style, my Jewish friends, my black friends, my Catholic sons-in-law, my agnosticism, and my left-of-center politics. I do hope, however, that he would admire my craftsmanship because in large measure I owe that to him.

One of my fondest memories of my days with him is a little rhyme that he taught me, which I now pass on to my students. It goes like this:

> *When a job is first begun*
> *Never leave it till it's done.*
> *Be the labor large or small*
> *Do it well or not at all.*

Bob had been a medic in World War II. When he came out of the service, he went to work for Fillauer Surgical Supply in Chattanooga. His territory was eastern Tennessee and southern Kentucky, which he worked from Monday till Friday. Every now and then he came home early on Thursday night. My brother and I always knew because from our bedroom we would see the lights come on in their backyard and hear their dog, Lady, barking.

Bob and Velma's backyard connected to ours by way of my uncle Floyd's backyard. Floyd was a member of the Ku Klux Klan and rode shotgun for the Hamilton County chain gang. The whole tract of backyards ran fifty or sixty yards from west to east, although it seemed a lot longer back then.

The plot our little five-room house stood on, like the plots of all the houses of my aunts and uncles, was at one time part of my maternal grandfather's land. His name was Will Haggard. He owned a grocery store on Shallowford Road, and like his son, he was a Klansman. Over time he parceled his land, giving plots to his son and his daughters to build their homes on.

The house next door to ours to the east was separated from ours by the scant width of a driveway and was the only house in that block and on that side of Shallowford Road that did not belong to a descendent of Will Haggard. It also had the only fenced-in backyard on that whole, long tract of land. That house belonged to the Whitmire family and according to my mother it had been built over the old pigsty. The result of this was that the Whitmires had the most fertile soil of all the yards. Their backyard was a veritable jungle of sunflowers, foxgloves, gladiola, and all sorts of vegetables. With all that fine old hog manure long in the soil to nourish them, things grew tall and verdant. Nothing grew in our yard except a couple of shrubs, a few jonquils, and some pink four-o'clocks that blossomed every summer afternoon alongside the driveway.

If it hadn't been for the Whitmire's fences, my brother and I and our friends would have been able to run and throw balls and play cowboys and Indians from aunt Annie Lee's house on one corner to Bob and Velma's on the other.

Bob and Velma's house was the largest and nicest of all our houses. It was the Haggard homestead, and was built around the turn of the century at the eastern foot of Missionary Ridge. Across the street to the west was grandaddy Haggard's grocery store. It's gone now, but it was still a grocery store when I was a little boy during the 1940s. Velma ran the store while Bob was away at Fort Benjamin Harrison. I remember that the screen door on the broad front porch had a "Colonial is Good Bread" push plate on it and a long spring that slapped it shut against the flies. There was a bright orange Orange Crush cooler with ice and cold bottled cokes of all sorts in it. It sat beneath one of the two big windows that had shutters on them. I remember a two-tiered candy case just inside the screen doors that faced the street and cordoned off the area where the cash register was. It had curved glass that seemed to warp everything inside it. Tommy used to crawl up into it to hide or steal candy and get fussed at when he got caught. The wooden floorboards were always cool and dusty and sagged under our little bare feet. At the back of the store there was a white porcelain-coated meat cooler that had a glass front. There was a big meat slicer and some white porcelain scales that sat on top of it alongside a roll of brown paper and a spindle of twine. Beyond all that was the back room where the walk-in ice-box was, and where the barrels of flour and pickles and crackers were kept.

The backyard of the Haggard store was off-limits to my brother and me. I don't know why. Perhaps the land didn't belong to the Haggards, or perhaps it was because it was all overgrown and there was an open abandoned well, which I was told was full of snakes. Of course, we played there anyway. Sometimes I would pretend to be Gene Autry & Champ or Roy Rogers & Trigger, and ride up to that old well, lean over it and spit or throw something in, and then run like mad through the briars and brambles to get away before getting caught. When the sun retreated behind Missionary Ridge, the trees and branches turned into monstrous shapes looming against the Mercurochrome sky.

There were other backyards too. Like Jimmy and Dickie Livingood's. Their backyard was fragrant with honeysuckle and fruit trees, and a long stretch of woods climbed off to the west, beyond the house. We were forbidden to play there because old man Tillett, or whatever his name was, lived back in there somewhere. We were told that he didn't like kids and so we convinced ourselves that if we got too close he might come out of his shack and shoot us. Beyond the Tillett place was a Baptist church that was forbidden territory too because it was a Negro church. It was full of mystery to us little white boys, and we never ventured close to it, even though

I knew that my mother's friend Vernita went to services there, and I knew somewhere deep in my heart that I had nothing to fear. But we played in those woods anyway. Played with toy guns and knives and bows and arrows. Battled our imaginary foes till dusk, fearless and brave, until the ancient crepuscular monsters began to come out of their lairs, and we ran home, exhilarated with fear and filthy from battle. Home to hot baths, supper, and the tranquility of sleep.

Some of the men in my family had been real soldiers. Some had fought real battles. Others merely served their time. Bob, as I said, was a medic. Wayland Moore, my cousin, was a navigator in the Army Air Corps, but got into the service too late to see action. Floyd drove an ambulance during the First World War and had a bad time of it from what we were told. We forever attributed his violent and mercuric personality to having been "shell-shocked." Daddy's brother, David, fought with Patton in Italy. Daddy himself couldn't pass the Army's physical because he was diabetic, but since he was an outstanding horseman he was called upon to teach horsemanship to the mounted troops of the Seventh Cavalry stationed at Fort Oglethorpe, Georgia.

War and tales of war were always part of my family, going back to the Civil War. I can trace it through my paternal grandfather, Albert LaFayette Moser, by way of a letter his brother wrote to my father. I am going to include part of that letter here, but first I must tell you a little more history.

My father's name was Arthur Boyd Moser. He was a professional gambler, a craps shooter as the family stories have it, though his profession as recorded on my birth certificate was "clerk." Regardless of how he made his money, Arthur Boyd and his pretty little wife, Wilhelmina, my mother, were well off in the 1930s partly due to an inheritance from Albert Moser's estate, and in larger part to the winnings at the craps table in Chattanooga and Chicago. Apparently Arthur squandered his money on Mother, cars, and on the accouterments of a nouveau-riche life. He drove a black Buick convertible that was decked out with a radio and whitewall tires. He bought

Mother furs and diamonds. He himself wore tailor-made clothes—more out of necessity than vanity, I suspect, because he was six foot three and weighed 300 pounds. He and Mother lived in a nice four-room apartment in a building on 3rd Street at Georgia Avenue. They employed a uniformed maid, whom my mother summoned with a little silver bell.

Their good living came to an abrupt end on September 19, 1941 when 31 year old Arthur Boyd succumbed to a malignant brain tumor in Atlanta. He left Mother the house he had built for her on her father's land, a black Buick convertible, and two baby boys. I was ten months old when he died. Mother's friend Vernita moved off her hill and came to live with us for a while, helping Mother take care of us boys. Three years later Mother married my step-father, Chesher Holmes. I loved Chesher and I always called him Daddy.

Arthur Boyd's father, Albert, was a grocerman like my grandaddy Haggard. His store stood on the corner of Vine and Third Street in Chattanooga. He was a 1909 graduate of Sweetwater College, which later became Tennessee Military Institute. While he was at Sweetwater, he was named the "Best Drilled Cadet in the Cadet Corps" and for this distinction he was awarded a ceremonial dress sword. Albert had a brother named George about whom very little is known. All I know about him is what can be inferred from this letter he wrote to Arthur Boyd about that ceremonial sword.

The letter was written in Detroit and is dated July 15, 1932, 1:15 pm—nine years before Arthur's death.*

It is addressed to "My dear Nephew:—".

And it begins:

"This is a long story and before you learn the whole of it you will be a very old man, if you live to be a wise and an old man, and if you don't, it doesn't matter.

---

* This letter was published by Pennyroyal Press in 1979 under the title *A Family Letter*. The syntax and punctuation has been preserved.

"In your veins runs the blood of Bailey, of Brown, of Snyder, of Brake-bill and of Moser. The last is not the most valuable, but even at that it is good blood. Your ancestors worked hard to get as far in the world of property and intelligence as they have come. They suffered many misfortunes and set-backs that would have broken the spirit of lesser breeds of poorer value. They suffered the crime of the reconstruction period of the civil war, they lost their property in that dastardly crime. The property loss is not worth mentioning, but there was much greater loss sustained, and I am prone to believe, that some of our Aunts and Uncles, (your great ones) endured this debasement and degradation too sweetly, they didn't resist as womanly and manly as they might have done. But that is not to be discussed here. You Grand-Father Moser did fairly well, perhaps as well as any Moser could have done, but he did not do well enough, he had to be helped by your Grand Mother Moser, your great-Uncle Jake, and Dr. Linn Bachman of Sweetwater, Tenn."

George goes on a bit about Arthur's grandfather, his Uncle Will, his Aunt Hestor. He tells him how dumb and provincial they all were and criticizes their lack of ambition. Then he says:

"So your Daddy (Albert) went to school in the smallest hick town in America. He was a kid chuck full of energy, he admired his teachers, he loved Bachman. He wasn't very bright, but he was one of the hardest workers who ever handled a knife, a shovel, a plow, a horse, or a blackjack... He could throw better than most men could shoot, he could jump better than all the boys he grew up with, he won prizes for jumping straight into the air and kicking at a target in the same movement. He was ambitious, and had his father have had one tenth of the money you have wasted since your Daddy died he would have gone to West Point, he would have today been one of the most efficient Officers in the United States Army...

"...Your Daddy had sand, and he tried ... your Daddy was a whiz.

"...he saved his first thousand of dollars when he was making twenty-five dollars a month, and when he finally got to the place where he was making a dollar per day, he couldn't even get his feet on the earth, he had wings of achievement pulling him off the earth. He took me with him ever so often to look at hogs, look at sows, look at white hogs. White hogs were his weakness, and white hogs finally destroyed him. He had a business head and he could make business pay him tribute, he could not work people, but he could work and do as much work as dozen people. This was the secret of whatever success he had. He forgot to play. He played more than his share when he was young, but as he grew older he grew dumber. He never could do more than one thing at a time. When he ran he ran to win; when he wrestled, he wrestled to win; whenever he kicked he kicked to win; whenever he drilled he drilled to win. You and your Mother buried his body in the grave of St. Elmo, but his soul is yet above the soil and I am taking it away from you. His soul is his sword. It is the only thing he ever loved, with one exception (that exception was you, and I swear this moment, that you are going to prove worthy of his living and his dying love) When I was a kid seven—ten—twelve years old I used to sit by him every Sunday, in the morning or in the afternoon, in the room where he and you uncle Will slept, fought, wrote, and strove to improve themselves. He would take that sword from the bowels of his old trunk, remove the cloth covering, remove the scabbard, and then he would polish that sword, as though it needed polishing; it never needed polishing any more than old Brin needed food, and do you think old Brin ever went hungry? I don't know whether I love the sword, your daddy, or that courageous dog the most, but all three of them are thoroughbreds, and a thorough-bred is always loved by me. He would let it lay on the bed for hours, and then after his soul and eyes were feasted to their content, he would replace everything in its place, then tenderly as a mother with her baby, he would place that sword in its proper place.

"...you see sonny boy, your Daddy was a soldier, he was trained to be a soldier, and he couldn't be nothing else. Can you imagine a soldier being a grocer man? Can you see, can you understand the tragedy of the whole thing? Everybody was in their wrong place; the civil war placed them below the negroes and they had a hard time living, much harder time trying to get back to the place where masterful white men should be, ought to be and are going to be. So he fought himself to death, he died of a broken heart, and he died knowing that he wasted his whole life, for he had to leave you when you most needed him. You know honey boy, you are a Brakebill, you are not a Moser. You are just like Aunt Amanda, Aunt Rachel; Aunt Matt, Uncle John. You want to live, you want to enjoy, you want to waste...."

Then he tells Arthur Boyd to prove himself "worthy of such a fighting, determined, courageous, brave, saving, honest, loving, striving Daddy," and if he doesn't, he says, "I will hound you out of the country. I will do it with a club like your Daddy chased his enemies out of his store with, and I will have a dog like unto our beloved Brin, snapping at your heels every time you touch your bleeding feet to the weeping earth ... get back to the land, get a place that is not too poor, get a place that has woods, water and hills and honeysuckle, cherries, and peaches and apples, get back to work and do something with that ox body of yours. You will starve to death and die cowardly if you do not do this.

"And send me your daddy's sword. And this is the way I want you to prepare it for shipment. It is your daddy's soul. So do him this courtesy: make a little case for it, make it look as much like a coffin as you can: Line it with gray, and cover the exterior parts with black, trim it with marigold and daisies. Spend a little of his money of him who lived his life entirely in vain; express the achievement to me.

"And when you have become a worthy son of my striving brother I shall return it to you; I shall return with it a thousand dollars for every pound it weighs; I will give you along with it a hundred dollars for every inch it is long.

"...Do as I have commanded you to do, and the next time I see you I don't want you to have one extra pound of lazy fat about that fine body of yours, I want you to be straight like your Daddy's drilling made him, I want you to die courageously, and if you do so you will have to live courageously. If you prove yourself a man, you shall have the sword, if not, it shall not have the dishonor of being in your possession. I am going to wear that sword this summer as I preach and speech to the people of this Nation. Swords are made for fighters, and they are not made for keep sakes, or play things. I am the personification of this Nation, the genius of this Nation is Activity, so get into motion. I hope that I may live to see the time when I can return it to you in the same way it was given to your Daddy, it will be a thing worth living to see. Love to you and to your wife and Mother.

"Uncle George

"Signing off at 3:15 pm"

Albert Moser's sword is still in Tennessee—with my brother. Along with much of the racism and bigotry expressed in his letter. The miasma of war, as you can see from this letter, shrouded my family. To them, war was noble and manly. From them I inherited the taint of bellicosity that ran in the Moser blood.

By World War II, all the Moser men were dead, though I'm not sure about George. Albert's wife, Evie, my grandmother, lived in a second floor apartment on McCallie Avenue. I sometimes went there on Saturdays to spend the night. I slept in the front room and lay awake watching the moving patterns of light on the ceiling from the headlights of cars passing on the street below. We went to church the next morning at Centenary Methodist. I loved and admired my Grandmother. She was a seamstress and worked with her hands like Bob. I especially adored her sister, Minnie Smith, who colored in coloring books with me. She was neat and delicate, and always, always, stayed inside the lines. Grandmother and Minnie let me stomp tin cans flat for the war effort. I remember that as I stomped I was told to sing out something like "Mash a can, kill a Jap! Mash a can, kill a Jap! Mash a can, kill a Jap!"

Most Saturdays, though, I stayed home and played in the backyard with my brother and our friends. We acted out scenes from movies we had been to—our imaginations fired by Superman, Hopalong Cassidy, John Wayne, and Frank Lovejoy. We played at being Supermen and Batmen and soldiers.

I even played war when I was alone.

When it rained, I staged cliff battles with toy soldiers and jeeps and tanks, carving out roads and caves in the dirt walls down in the basement. When it was sunny, I staged battles in the backyard. I made scores of soldiers out of modeling clay. I preferred them to the static plastic ones I bought at the ten cent store because I could change their poses and gestures.

I staged air battles from the back stoop. Building model airplanes was, it would seem, the primary purpose of my boyhood. It caused me to be something of a dunce in elementary school because I was always day-dreaming about the Spitfire or Mustang or Black Widow I was working on back at home—dreaming up ways to make the instrument panel more realistic or how to attach bombs that would drop or how to make rivet patterns or how to make the canopy slide. The sliding canopy or rivet pattern was frequently interrupted by Mrs. Collett or Mrs. Turner saying, "BARRY! I asked if you did your homework?"

"No, ma'am."

"Well, why not?"

"I dunno."

I never confessed to the countless hours I spent working on model airplanes at the expense of reading, writing, and arithmetic.

The models themselves were never very good, because, as Bob frequently told me, I was too impatient to get the thing built so that I could fawn over the details. This is a serious flaw in a craftsman and it took me many years to learn that and to overcome it. I still struggle with it from time to time.

When I finished a model, I hung it from the ceiling with a tack and some thread, and then laid down on my bed underneath it and imagined myself in its cockpit. I flew it on flights of fancy, if you will—dangerous and courageous missions full of death-defying dives and spiraling victory rolls. Every now and again I stood up on the bed and changed the model's attitude and laid down again and did it all over. When I grew tired of a plane I painted enemy insignias on it, squeezed some glue on the tail section or in the cockpit, set it afire, and sailed it off the back stoop to crash and burn in the backyard.

More than anything in the world I wanted to be an aviator. The dream of becoming a flyer stayed alive all the way through military school. It wasn't until I was a freshman at Auburn that the reality of my eyesight brought home the fact that I would never be able to qualify for flight school.

As a result, my life changed and I went into directions that at that time I could never have dreamed of.

The toy wars of my backyard continued when I went to Baylor in 1952 and put on that gray uniform I wore to Bob's funeral and was issued a toy wooden rifle with which to learn the School of the Soldier and the Manual of Arms. I was eleven. We were issued M-1 carbines in the 9th grade. I was thirteen years old then and had to memorize the serial number, learn how to field strip it, how to clean it, and how to put it back together again without having any parts left over. We learned how to fire the M-1 when we got to be seniors—on an Army shooting range in Chattooga, Georgia. I didn't do very well. I won no medals.

I won no medals for drawing either, because there were no art courses at Baylor at that time, and getting caught drawing during study hall was reason for reprimand and sometimes even a sound paddling.

I was promoted to the rank of Cadet Lieutenant in my senior year—a rank which was pretty much the lowest rank a six-year senior like myself could make. Becoming a cadet officer required that I carry a saber and that I learn the Manual of the Saber, which is to say that I had to learn how to salute and march with it. That saber rests today on the mantle in my library alongside a set of Shakespeare I designed for Doubleday Book & Music Club and a Little League bat signed to me by Willie Morris, a memento of our collaboration on *A Prayer for the Opening of the Little League Season*.

My saber is a keepsake, a memento, like that bat. It reminds me that in my family and the society of my youth, a man was judged to be a man by his guns, knives, and swords—not his love of art or poetry, and certainly not by his library. Today I hope and trust that my stature as a man is and will be judged by my art and by my books. But—even if that be so, it does not contravene the fact that I am who I am because I was refined through the fires of my own particular and unique history and experience—an early mentor, a racist family, military school, thirty years of teaching, rearing my own family, and what now seems like a lifetime of studying and practicing my art and my craft, polishing it over and over like my grandfather polished his beloved sword.

Palimpsest

A few years ago a newspaper reporter asked me what I thought my most important work was. She was expecting that I would answer with a title of one of the books I've illustrated—*Alice, Moby-Dick, Jump! The Adventures of Br'er Rabbit*. But I responded, "Being a good father."

"No, no, no," she said, "That's not what I mean."

"Oh, well then," I said, "having been a good teacher."

"No, no," she insisted. "I mean…"

I interrupted her and said, "I know what you mean, but you see, what you're looking for plays pretty far down the line in my hierarchy of things important." What did I mean by that? I have no intention of expounding on what a good teacher is, but for me it means this:

One, I like kids.

Two, I always try to teach kids and not courses.

Three, I try to be selfless enough with my kids so as not to cheat them out of my honesty or out of whatever else I have that I can give them.

Four, I consider myself a servant—it is their class, after all, not mine.

And, five, I try to be ever-vigilant in the encouragement of individuality, non-conformity, and freedom of expression. And I try to be ever mindful of potential emotional, intellectual, and artistic suicides—those dreadful and unfortunate moments, largely unnoticed, when the delicate, embryonic ember of thought, reason, and creativity are snuffed out by a casual or cruel or negatively critical comment.

Needless to say, I caused my administration a good deal of consternation.

But this talk is not about education and teaching. It is about my family, about my childhood, and about the environment which surrounded my childhood. For mine, you see, was a growing-up in which the embers of independence, non-conformity, and creativity were very nearly snuffed out.

My family was made up of people who were members of the Ku Klux Klan and bulwarks of their churches. There were grocermen and traveling salesmen. There were housewives who stayed home, smoked cigarettes, and complained. There was an uncle who wasn't talked about much because he had had syphilis and his son, my cousin, was born blind as a cause of it.

My father, Arthur Boyd Moser, died of a brain tumor when I was 10 months old, and my mother, who was a typical southern housewife, remarried when I was two. She married a man named Chesher Holmes who sold sporting goods and who later managed the Chattanooga Golf and Country Club. He was my daddy. None of us were poor, not like the "white trash" at which we looked down our noses. We never lacked for food or clothing and all our houses were comfortably furnished.

My family took care to see that I was brought up "properly"—which is to say that I was taught to be obedient, taught how to handle guns, how to play all the right sports (football, etc.), how to hunt and fish, to stand up and to say "yes ma'am" and "yes sir," to think of doctors as gods, and to revere the military. To their immense pride I graduated from a prestigious military academy (whose assessment of me—as captioned under my senior picture in the yearbook, the 1958 Kliff Klan—was that "Moser is never on top in any field.")

But, despite the fact that I dress conservatively, still say "yes sir" and "yes ma'am," still stand out of respect when an older person or woman enters the room or comes to the table—my family (or what's left of it) has difficulty with my liberal political mind, my distrust of their beloved and revered religious leaders, my distaste for war and the military, and my complete disinterest in football.

The place I speak of is East Tennessee—Chattanooga—and the time I speak of is the 1940s and 50s. My family were not readers. My mother read *The Reader's Digest* and novels like *Forever Amber*. My father read the *Chattanooga Times* and the *Chattanooga News-Free Press*. My aunt Velma read Mary Baker Eddy's *Science and Health with Keys to the Scriptures*. And some of them read the Bible. I didn't read anything. I don't even remember anyone reading to me except in school. I remember reading (or looking at) *Little Black Sambo* with the girl who lived next door, Vanova Whitmire. More than likely it was her book, not mine. And I am sure that we were encouraged to read when we played with Jimmy and Dickie Livingood, because their father was a professor at the University of Chattanooga and they did things like that. I am equally sure that I had books, but the only ones I remember having were the first two volumes of *The Standard American Encyclopedia*, A to Art and Art to Boo. These I remember vividly because there, between A and Art, was an entry for "Anatomy" which was illustrated with a photograph of a "transparent woman" and a drawing of a man whose belly was splayed open exposing his entrails. A flap of abdominal skin hung down over his privates like a loin cloth. His empty eyes were wide-spaced, black and surly, like a Pentecostal preacher.

I went back to see him again, that "Anatomy-man" side-show freak, a specter that haunted the sparse living room bookshelf, my bedroom closet, the underside of my bed, and my dreams. I suppose "Anatomy-man" was instrumental in my interest in dissection in high school biology, in my taking a minor in biology at the university, in my interest in medical and natural anomalies, and in my penchant for making pictures for books (having a predilection for the grotesque). I still have those two books. And today "Anatomy-man" is tucked away, between A and Boo, quiet and unnoticed in my library—squeezed in among tomes on anatomy, anomalies, diseases of the skin, plastic and reconstructive surgery, surgery of the eye, and animal castration.

While I remember looking at the Anatomy entry, I don't remember reading it, because, you see, I looked, I didn't read. And I looked at everything, at "Anatomy-man," at *Look*, at *The Saturday Evening Post*, at *Life*. I looked at Marvel Comics and Classics Illustrated. These were my books. I drew and traced the characters: Jean Valjean, Hawkeye and Uncas, Superman, Captain America and Captain Marvel, Archie and Jughead. And on the weekends, or evenings, when no one was home, I made tracings of Betty and Veronica without their clothes on. Certainly my abiding interest in drawing, painting, and engraving the human figure can be traced to Betty and Veronica.

Saturdays, when I didn't stay home tracing Betty and Veronica, I went to the movies at the State Theater, the Tivoli, The Rialto, the Brainerd. These were my stories: Hopalong Cassidy, the Cisco Kid, Johnny Mack Brown, Roy Rogers and Gabby Hayes. *Abbott and Costello Meet Frankenstein* was the first movie that scared me. I remember the sticky floor of the theater where I cowered from Lon Chaney Jr.'s werewolf. My mother took me to see Walt Disney's *The Song of the South* which introduced me to Br'er Rabbit and Br'er Fox (I remember wearing knickers); she took me to see his *Pinocchio* too, whom I loved so much I named my little toy bulldog after him; and of course I saw *Snow White and the Seven Dwarfs*.

When I went to college in 1958, I was thinking that someday I might go to California and become an animator for Disney or, better still, for Warner Brothers. I loved drawing animals and figures in the slap-happy animator's style and I did so, it seems, endlessly. I painted a big confederate soldier on the wall of my room in my fraternity house who looked an awful lot like Yosemite Sam. And when I became a new father five years later, I did a large oil painting of Br'er Bear and hung it in my daughter's nursery to celebrate her birth and to look over her. He was an Appalachian bear, with bare feet and coveralls, brandishing a bouquet and a bludgeon. He now hangs in my granddaughters' nursery and looks over them when they visit "Bubba."

I learned a lot from drawing like that—I learned to draw quickly, to exaggerate features, and how to overstate expressions, especially eyes. But, above all, I learned gesture—the capturing of the essence of a subject rather than its surface and appearance. And I think, today, that gesture is the seminal lesson for all artists, be they poets, painters, or musicians.

In 1985, Bonnie Verburg, then an editor at Harcourt Brace Jovanovich, asked me to illustrate a new adaptation of five Br'er Rabbit stories, which she had on her desk. I was reluctant, being attached (as only a very few people are) to the Joel Chandler Harris renderings. I suspected this new "adaptation" of bowdlerization. But happily, Van Dyke Parks brought his musical ear and his Mississippi memory to bear on his adaptations, and rendered them honestly and truly. And before long I set about illustrating my first children's book: *Jump!* (HBJ, 1986). The illustrations were humorous, anthropomorphic animal figures similar to the ones I had done in college: Br'er Fox and Br'er Rabbit, Br'er Bear and Br'er Wolf. That was a great discovery for me—or rediscovery, as it were—and proved to be a turning point in my work.

On the one hand *Jump!* gave venue and authority to the lighter side of my artistic personality, long neglected while illustrating Melville, Dante, Homer, and Virgil. It touched those distant and pleasant times of "funny books," cartoons, and movies. Br'er Rabbit wanted color and a light spirit. He wanted sparklin' eyes an' dancin' feet. Inventing him was the first step in the reunification of my adult consciousness with long forgotten memories of childhood and the first step in a difficult process of integrating my past with my present work. The settings I invented for Hominy Grove are far more intimate to me and my heritage than the settings I invented for Victorian England, Renaissance Italy, Ancient Greece, or Ishmael's sea.

In his Gospel, St. John suggests that we, "Gather up the fragments that remain so that nothing is lost." But how does one gather fragments which are so far out of mind, and which one has tried to forget? Most of my family is dead. I can't ask them, now that I have the questions to ask, now that I want to know. And I don't trust my memory because I suspect that much of it is conjured from seeing family photographs and/or from hearing stories told over and over.

I love family photographs—not only pictures of my own family but anonymous family photographs as well. I find the sense of drama about them appealing—the universal drama of "family" frozen, as it were, in light, time, and incident. I would note two recent books where I used family photographs as bases for illustration: one, a photograph of my brother, Tommy, standing on the front porch of our grandaddy Haggard's grocery store on Shallowford Road, became the image of "Boyd" in Cynthia Rylant's *Appalachia, The Voices of Sleeping Birds* (HBJ, Spring, 1991); and another, a picture of my mother's stove, became Jahdu's oven in Virginia Hamilton's *The All Jadhu Storybook* (HBJ, Fall, 1992).

Anyway, I was a quiet child—for the most part anyway. I had friends and playmates, and was probably as gregarious as any other boy, but I was different in that I enjoyed my solitude as much as I enjoyed the camaraderie of my friends and playmates. In many ways I was happiest when I was alone because that was when I drew and listened to music. Not much has changed, though I'm not as quiet as I was when I was a boy.

The one contact with art I had as a child was with music. We had a Victrola phonograph that was so tall I had to stand on a chair to put the old 78 rpm records on it, one at a time. There were recordings of Enrico Caruso, John Charles Thomas, George Gershwin, Eddie Duchin, The Ink Spots, Fats Waller, Ted Lewis. A film, *Song Without End*, in which Cornel Wilde played Frederick Chopin introduced me to Chopin's music, and showed me one of the most arresting pictorial compositions in my memory—a drop of bright vermilion blood plashing on the black and white keyboard of the piano. Chopin was the first musical love of my life, in fact the first record I ever bought was a recording of the *A Major Polonaise*. I don't remember who played it, perhaps Arthur Rubinstein.

Saturday afternoons, when I wasn't at the movies or tracing Betty and Veronica, I listened to the Metropolitan Opera on the radio while I drew or built model airplanes. It is little wonder that words like timbre, rhythm, cadence, *pochissimo*, *fortissimo*, and so forth, are frequent terms in my critical vocabulary and in my verbalizing of what I do.

Sometimes on Saturdays though, I invented wars for my toy soldiers and my model airplanes.

But, mostly, I drew on Saturdays. And painted. I drew and painted pictures on brown wrapping paper my daddy brought home from work, and I drew on the cardboard from his laundered shirts. I drew on whatever I could find—on butcher paper and freezer paper, on stationery somebody had taken from a hotel in Lexington or Atlanta, or on rolls of adding machine paper. And when I could find nothing else, I tore off pieces of waxed paper and made tracings. I drew Roman gladiators and Royal Canadian Mounted Police, animals and airplanes (often carrying "Atommy" bombs, which I spelled A-t-o-m-m-y, because I thought it had something to do with my brother, Tommy). I drew cowboys and Indians, and ships at sea, and of course, I drew naked figures. Many years later my daddy told me that I shouldn't paint pictures of "nekkid" women because he was afraid that the headmaster of the school where I was teaching, the McCallie School in Chattanooga, would find out about it and fire me.

We told stories in my family, like all families did before television, stories about the cousins over in Decherd; about the white woman up in the hollow who lived next door to black folks and who nursed her babies until they were too old to nursed; about the "white trash" who lived behind us on Rockway Drive; and about the people who lived across the street and who got drunk Saturday nights and set about screaming and hollering and throwing things at each other. I can hear my daddy telling stories on Sunday afternoon "drives" over to Copper Hill or down to Sand Mountain, and if our ride brought us home after dark and along lower Shallowford Road, he would tell us his tale about a "headless haint" who haunted the road where it passed through a dark stretch of woods and would, he said, fly up into our headlights "like a sheet."

The family stories were told and retold, embellished and altered by dint of the memory and imagination of whoever was doing the telling, so that the stories came to exist in several versions. ("No, no, no ... t'wern't Aunt Velma a'tall, it wuz Aunt Grace did that.") Ultimately the story itself survived, not the particulars.

Something else happened as I listened to my aunts and uncles talk and tell stories: I learned to speak Pig-Latin. My folks spoke it rapidly when they wanted to say something they didn't want me to here, like eyeshay eemcray (Pig-Latin for ice cream). I listened to my folks on quiet summer evenings, Sundays usually, when we gathered on Velma's screened-in porch. Her old metal glider, upholstered in green and white striped canvas, squeaked with age—as did her green, scalloped-shaped lawn chairs which we had brought in from badminton to get away from the bugs which now buzzed at the screen trying to get at the floor lamps which glowed through amber-colored paper shades. Paper fans with wooden handles and portraits of Jesus on them lay here and there. A hooked rug covered the gray painted floor. African violets flourished in white, curlicue stands near the front door. I remember the tightness of my belly, full of Sunday dinner: fried chicken and milk gravy; turnip greens and buttermilk biscuits; a water-melon more than likely—a round one, like a cannonball, dark Hooker's green, which my uncle Bob would have plugged in the afternoon to make sure it was ripe and had immersed in a tub of ice to make sure it was cold enough to eat. Or homemade ice cream or, best of all, peach cobbler made with fresh Georgia Belle peaches.

Eventually I learned to speak Pig-Latin fluently and rapidly like my aunts and uncles, and in doing so, I think the first seeds of my interest in language were planted: language as play, language as structure, language as an aware-ness of words, language as entertainment—we, my brother and I, had no idea of how Pig-Latin was structured, but God, how we would hoot with laughter trying to figure out what they were saying, and getting our tongues wrapped around all that delicious nonsense.

Heraclitus said that "In the tension of opposites, all things have their being." Nowhere in my memory is this more apparent than in my memory of language. The day-to-day language of my family (which does not include the wonderful, though fanatical, writing of my father's uncle George, which Eudora Welty has admired for its unabashed strength), however rurally poetic it may have been, was not elegant. Nor was it literate. Rather, it was common and bigoted. Aunts and uncles, mother and father said things like "That woman never did have no common sense did she?" and "That dog shore does like to chase 'coons, don't he?" And it goes without saying that there were no foreign languages spoken in my family, except Pig-Latin, because they were skeptical of all foreign things, including Unitarians, Congregationalists, Jews, Catholics, and of course, ALL people of color. The anecdotes of my uncles, the playful Pig-Latin of my aunts, and even the sweetness of my mother's loving voice comforting me from the despair of a nightmare, are diminished in my memory today by their seemingly ubiquitous language of hate and bigotry.

I see my childhood now as having been marred by these verbal stains. At that time I had no consciousness of the stains, nor any notion that these stains would, later in life, become scars. I never questioned or challenged my family when they told me that "niggers ain't human" and that "Jews ain't much better," and that "Catholicks worship idols." I didn't question or challenge because I was a polite and obedient child. But I remember that I never understood their hate, and I never accepted it. Their hate never turned to blood or bile in me. And I never understood why I couldn't sit in the back of the bus when black folks were sitting there (would they hurt me?), or why I couldn't drink from water fountains marked "colored" (would I catch something?), or why I couldn't kiss my mother's black friend, Vernita (would the black rub off?).

As I grew older and first began questioning and then ultimately rejecting my family's values, and the values of military school, I became aware of other prejudices as well: against artists and intellectuals, for instance, and against people who tacked contrary to the family—like me, for marrying "a Yankee bitch" (from Missouri); and against anyone who held a different concept of the Almighty God from the one they embraced and which they *knew* without a doubt to be The Truth. By the time I was twenty-seven, I had grown uncomfortable in Chattanooga, or at least with my perception of Chattanooga, and (like a latter-day Huck Finn) lit out for New England—and became an expatriate southerner.

"Experience is never limited," Henry James said, "and it is never complete; it is a kind of huge spider-web of the finest silken threads suspended in the chamber of consciousness and catches every air-borne particle in its tissue." Now, twenty-three years later, the memories and scars of my childhood experiences have begun to arise from the ashes and, like Dante on the banks of Lethe, the river of forgetfulness, I find myself with a new muse, one who says to me as she said to the Florentine, "I have come ready for all your questions till you are satisfied."

That was how the month began.

It ended with the cold, passionless fuck of a whore. The coming together of two bodies that was not a covenant of the flesh but a betrayal of the flesh. The taste was not of sun-warmed berries but of meat gone bad.

It happened at a party. I had invited fifteen friends to dinner. The dress was black tie. The invitation was handset and printed letterpress using the mome rath from the as-yet unpublished Pennyroyal *Looking-Glass* as an illustration. It was supposed to be a feast, a wayzgoose in the wrong season. The caterers served up a whole roasted pig with an apple in its mouth and all the appropriate trimmings. Tables were set up in the press room and dressed in linen and silver and decorated with arrangements of phallic Anthurium. I hired two women to dance and entertain. That was all. Black and white erotic videos played silently on a television set that was perched on the delivery of the old Kelly 2. Puccini and Verdi arias played on a stereo early in the evening, though by ten o'clock they had been usurped by Led Zeppelin and the Rolling Stones. And the dancers danced to that music, undressing, bit by bit, as the gentlemen in black tie ate pig and drank whiskey. We called our evening *Ars Porcinorum*, the art of the pig. And before the night was over, I was handing out money (recently earned by the success of *Alice*) by the fistfuls for the sexual favors the dancers ended up offering to my guests. The debauchery of that night set me on an unexpected and downwardly spiraling course of introspection that penetrated deep into an unknown and unfamiliar region where a self I did not know dwelt beneath the self I thought I knew so well.

When I was a boy I used to explore a cave outside South Pittsburgh, Tennessee. It was called Nick-a-Jack and was used as a saltpeter mine and a hide-out for war-weary confederate troops during the Civil War. My friends and I used to go there often. Sometimes we just hung out at the mouth of the cave, smoking cigarettes and lying about girls. Other times we packed spelunking gear and explored Nick-a-Jack's bowels. On more than one occasion we got lost (or thought ourselves lost) in its cool and total darkness. Charlie Winger sometimes rigged a ball of twine on a toilet paper dispenser and fastened the contraption to his belt so that it would pay out the twine so we could follow it back and find our way out, especially if we were planning a deep exploration.

One time the clue snagged and broke and Winger didn't notice. That time we were truly lost. Lost in the thick, silent blackness. Lost in the belly of the earth. We tried not to panic, tried not to act like the frightened little boys we were. We were all scared and we all knew it. But we blew ourselves up with as much bravado as we could pretend and boldly retraced our steps and explored new passageways. One such passageway was very tight, so tight and narrow that we had to crawl single-file. Then we had to go to our bellies. We were crawling towards the edge of what seemed to be a precipice, thinking it to be a precipice because our lights picked up nothing in the distance. Nothing but black air. As we elbowed our way to the edge, we saw an arrow scratched into the wall, pointing down. Above the arrow was the word: "HELL." Fright came instantly and unmitigated. Our heartbeats echoed and resonated in and among the tunnels and walls of old Nick-a-Jack who had undoubtedly heard it all before. Somebody cried. Somebody laughed. But we did come back out into the open. We always did, and we lay exhausted on the ground, drinking in the light and warm summer breezes, laughing as boys do to disguise and deny the fear we were ashamed to have revealed inside.

So it is with self-portraiture. I usually begin with the familiar surfaces of my face—with its planes and textures and idiosyncrasies—in much the same way that I explored the familiar river and the ledges and boulders of Nick-a-Jack's mouth. But there is no risk staying near the light. In not venturing into the silence of the unknown dark. And there is no risk in staying safely within the surface planes, textures, and features of a face and a body familiar to me from this side of the mirror, instead of staking out the perimeters, pushing the self toward darkness—evil or benign—if only to find out where the limits lie on the other side of the mirror. To find out where my limits are, to find where I cannot go again.

In the silence and dark of Nick-a-Jack, armed only with the cold, carbide light each of us carried alone, we were stripped to our essentials, and were carried forward by the thrill of our own adolescent madness toward the edge of fear, the edge of hell itself.

And so it is with the journey of self-portraits. But not always. Some journeys in self exploration are humorous and light-hearted. Some are merely factual—representations that mark the passing of time, the gaining of weight, and the thinning of hair. Others are dark and frightening. As a body of work they represent a solitary voyage like those of Ulysses, Æneas, Dante, Alice—a voyage on which only I could carry the light or pay out the clue. Like spelunking, the journey into the self required something of that all-but-forgotten egocentric, adolescent insanity I knew as a boy.

In the winter of 1983 I was preparing new work for a solo exhibit in New York City at Mary Ryan's gallery on Columbus Avenue. Most of the work was to be self-portraits, a plan that was established before Jane came into my life that February. I worked irrepressibly for the show, and as I did my obsession with her opened my mind up like a wound and the blood of my passion and lust for her triggered a fury of work—mostly self-portraits, mostly drawings, and mostly large-scale. Forty-seven pieces of that work were shown in the exhibit. But, then again, much of it—most of it?—was thrown away. Burned. Destroyed. And it was all done in twenty-eight days.

When my oldest daughter saw my studio filling up with the door-sized self-portraits, she said to me with the casual, know-it-all directness only teenagers show: "You sure do think a lot of yourself, don't you, Dad?"

Hurt, I snapped back at her: "If all you see is me, then you don't understand the self-portrait." By which I meant that through the exploration of the self, of one's face and one's shape, especially as one looks into the caves of one's own eyes, the artist begins to explore the recesses of all men, beasts, and gods. It was too much for an adolescent to comprehend. I continued my harangue nevertheless. I reminded her that each of us ultimately leaves his or her parents, either by choice or by death, just as our children must sooner or later leave us. I reminded her that we can leave our lovers or our spouses, too, for short periods of time or we can leave them for good. And I reminded her that with most of the people we meet in our lives, the question of leave-taking will be beside the point. But the truth is that we can never take leave of the self, for it is omnipresent and inescapable, and we better make our peace with it or else we have a very long row to hoe indeed. When, therefore, the artist begins to explore this terrain, he begins to explore the only omnipresent and universal world he will ever know.

I began those 1983 self-portraits playing with images familiar to me: the self as Bacchus and as Faunus. As Priapus, both *fortissimo* and *pochissimo*, because (in light of Jane) I felt comfortable with this sexual, half-pathetic, half-comic rutting self. But soon I began to explore other self-deformations and transfigurations as well. These are the masks all people wear at the most intimate level: masks of truth and masks of falsehood, masks of profanity and irreverence, masks of passion and desire, of empathy and celebration, the mask of the moral dwarf and the mask of the freak, the transfigurative masks of the saint and the martyr. And how many of us have not, like Satan, played with the masks of Christ and God?

Masks are like the sweet red flesh of the yew berry which covers its poisonous seed, the sweet illusion of immortality covering the very fact of mortality. And so a mask of the carnival freak and a mask of the dead Christ, a mask of the achondroplastic dwarf and a mask of the pierced Sebastian in his homoerotic passion, a mask of contempt we put on for the arrogant politician or the bigoted religionist, a mask of ribald humor, a mask of pathos and of pain—all enshrined in the husk which hides our own rotting deaths. For that which is corporeal will pass away, food for worms, as Zorba teaches us. Dust unto dust. But the Masks themselves, those manifestations of the artist's compassion and the universality of his humanity: these we hope, are immortal.

And yet, just as the yew berry's sweetness needs a savory, so I need the taste of truth. And what began as a playful interlude with myself (my *self*?) soon led downward into an Archimedean spiral which became more and more self-destructive. I had come to the edge of another abyss beyond which I could not go, another arrow pointing down toward Hell itself.

I took a week off the next month, a few days after *Ars Porcinorum*. I flew to Tortola for the sun. One day as I lay nearly naked on the beach, I began admiring, ogling really, a young blond woman. She was wearing a black bikini and her back was toward me. As if this fat man hadn't had enough of the flesh to last awhile, I fantasized about her in the strong afternoon light, sneaking furtive glances behind dark glasses. Peering at her above pages of Seamus Heaney. She got up to leave and when she reached for her tee-shirt I noticed that her forearms and hands were inverted and folded back on themselves. Thalidomide? How in God's name, I asked myself, could I explain my self-portrait as a carnival freak to this young woman with the deformed arms? Embarrassed and feeling pangs of guilt I buried my eyes back into *The Naturalist*. But I didn't read. I asked myself that question over and over. "I'm an artist," I heard myself answering each time, hoping that she would understand. Hoping that I would understand. For myself, I know that I have yet to drive the cold iron spikes of exploration into that part of myself which I saw reflected in that woman and the two dancers. All three were strangers to me, but they were all three mirrors in which I saw reflections of those elements of myself—beauty, ugliness, deformity. Then again, in them I might have met my muse, my trinity: god, man, and brute.

Now, these years later, having engraved and painted and drawn who knows how many more self-portraits, I have come to realize manifestly that we are, each of us, made up of many people and that we wear different masks at different times and in the company of different people. Self-portraits, like masks, are both concave and convex. Self-portraiture attempts to explore the masks of "I" that are worn both outwardly and inwardly. I never begin with the idea of Everyman, although I think I end there, because the man who explores himself explores the hearts of all men.

THERE WAS A TIME

A Talk Given at the Children's Literature Festival
The University of the Redlands
April 17, 1998

M<small>Y TALK THIS MORNING</small> has something in common with the many
sermons I gave back when I was putting myself through college as a licensed
Methodist preacher: it uses personal experience to make my point. Indeed,
one of the first principles I learned about effective preaching came from an
old preacher who told me that the best way to sway "all them sinners out
there" was to tell them real-life stories. In other words, to witness for Christ
through the power of personal experience. Now while I wouldn't have called
myself a Pentecostal back then, that's exactly what I was. Because my preaching was not only steeped in the reading of the Bible as the inerrant and infallible word of God, it also emphasized the paving of one's path to the
Almighty through the lessons of an individual life.

So this morning I will explore personal experience along this tack: I believe everything I have done in my life has played a part, large or small, in leading me to this place, to this time, and to the project I am currently working on. Like all the people you will hear during the course of this conference, I have arrived at this point in my career and in my life by way of unique, circuitous, and even aberrant routes. My journey is the subject of my talk this morning.

The theme of my comments, if there is one beyond the purely anecdotal, is this: if we, as artists, writers, students, and teachers don't grow and advance, we atrophy and die. We die as surely as a pupa dies if it becomes strangled by the silk of its own cocoon. For writers and illustrators of books, the silk is the silk of good reviews, an adoring public, and large advances. The cocoon is fashioned out of our subscribing to our public's admiration, believing our reviews, and accepting our present and persistent mediocrity as something beyond that because of the large advances. We must always bear in mind that everything—EVERYTHING—is mediocre as long as it can be done better than it has been done. To make this point, I will take you back through some of my own life experiences.

There was a time, fifty years ago, when I drew pictures of gladiators, Royal Canadian Mounted Police, cowboys and Indians, and, most of all, airplanes. My brother Tommy and I spread out large sheets of brown wrapping paper on the living room floor and drew air battles. We spent hours drawing ground troops and tanks and artillery, which served as targets for our high-flying bombers and daredevil fighters that we would add later on in our game.

My brother always drew better than I did. He was three years older than I and that may explain it—although I think that his natural meticulousness had as much to do with it as anything. When his bombers opened their bomb bays, the bombs fell away in straight, evenly spaced files. My bombs varied in size and fell back in an arc away from my bomber rather than in neatly spaced, perfectly vertical rows like his. They also fell in graduated stages from the horizontal to the vertical, which is, of course, the way a World War II bomb actually behaved. My drawings were clumsy and cluttered compared to my brother's, which were always clean, neat, and methodical.

The difference, as I see it now, was that my brother's drawings were informed by a sense of order—a perfectly valid point of view from which to work. My drawings, on the other hand, were informed by logic and observation, which is an equally valid point of view.

There was a time, later on, when I drew nothing but naked women. Naked men too (as with gladiators), but mostly naked women. This phenomenon, I am sure, was a naturally occurring manifestation of an eleven-year-old endocrine system that was just beginning to produce testosterone. I even made tracings of Betty and Veronica, taking their clothes off in the process. I don't remember ever making nude tracings of Archie or Jughead.

More than once I got into trouble at school for drawing naked women. One time was in the tenth grade. I was in a military school in Chattanooga. First Year Spanish. Winter term. Second period. Rain. The instructor was Señor René Bazan. As usual, I was not paying attention to the lesson. Instead I was locked within my own mind, listening to the rain, and contemplating the roundness of breasts as I drew them on a blank page of my textbook. I didn't see him approaching. When he saw what I was doing, he snapped me up by my shirt collar like a dog, and made me leave class and report to the Commandant, who made me empty my back pockets, bend over, and grab my ankles whereupon he took his "board of education" to my backside. But, alas, the lesson didn't stick. I still draw naked figures.

Then there was a time when I drew cartoons.

I went to college at Auburn University in 1958 thinking that maybe one day I would go work for Warner Brothers—drawing Foghorn Leghorn, the Tasmanian Devil, and the like. I decorated one of the walls of my room in the Kappa Alpha house with a large mural of a Yosemite Sam-type confederate miscreant holding a gun in one hand, a beer can in the other, and mouthing—in big letters—"Forget, Hell!"

Drawing cartoons taught me some very important lessons, which I still find useful—mostly about gesture, expressions, and exaggeration.

I can't say that there was a time when I drew letters because I've always drawn letters. One of the few pieces of my own work that hangs in my house is a rendering of a motto my Uncle Bob taught me forty-one years ago. It's lettered in a very decorative "Old English" on a 16 x 20 sheet of ordinary paper. The motto itself is not important, but I'll read it to you anyway just for flavor. It is titled *Why Worry?*

> *There are only two things to worry about.*
> *Either you are well or you are sick. If you are well then*
> *there is nothing to worry about, but if you are sick there*
> *are two things to worry about, either you'll get well*
> *or you'll die. If you get well there's nothing to worry about.*
> *If you die and go to heaven, then there's nothing to worry*
> *about. If you go to hell you'll be so busy shaking hands*
> *with old friends, you won't have time to worry.*

It is dated October 10, 1957, five days before my seventeenth birthday. I keep it hanging because it reminds me that at sixteen I was already in love with letters. Silly and un-craftsmanlike as it is, that prosaic broadside points towards the life with letters that I still live. Points toward that life despite the fact that it is badly executed—done by drawing each letter and filling them in rather than being properly written in three or four strokes with the broad-nibbed pen as was instructed in the Speedball lettering manual from which I copied the letterforms.

Looking back I can see that I have never taken formal lessons very well. Colonel Baker's board of education didn't stop me from drawing in class or study hall, nor did the fear of flunking out of college and becoming fodder for Vietnam make me read the books I was supposed to read nor do the drawings I was supposed to do. I do not mean to imply by this that I was an arrogant and difficult student. To the contrary, I was polite, easygoing, and tried honestly to do what was expected of me. It was just that I read too slowly to keep up with the reading requirements, so I didn't do them. In my drawing classes I was too preoccupied with what I could already do well—i. e., draw realistically—to be interested in learning anything I didn't already know.

I ended up teaching myself the things I needed and wanted to know after I was out of college. I have never had a course (night, university, or otherwise) in typography—which is my great love. Neither have I done formal, academic studies in book design, illustration, wood engraving, calligraphy, watercolor, or writing. I have learned what I know about the allied book arts by trial and error. By experiment and failure. William Faulkner said that "failure is worth while and admirable, provided only that the failure is splendid enough, the dream splendid enough, unattainable enough yet forever valuable enough, since it was of perfection."

Of all my self-taught lessons, though, the most difficult of all was overcoming my reluctance to learn to draw better than I already could and understanding, finally, that I was too good not to become better.

When I first went to college my "artistic" interests were strictly rooted in subject matter, in the close observation and imitation of nature. I think of this period of my life as my artistic adolescence—a kind of "look what I can do, Ma!" phase. I'm glad I didn't become arrested there as many of my stripe do. The temptation is very great once one has conquered that tedious little mountain of tricks called verisimilitude to stop at that level of achievement and go no further. Having achieved this seductive summit, one is tempted to heap upon it more and more detail which, more often than not, results in seeing everything in a picture in the same degree of focus and attention, in telling everything and asking nothing, in stating and not implying. To stop and rest here is to become a dilettante.

In 1960 my Auburn career hit a financial snag that sent me home and to the University of Chattanooga. There were only two instructors in the art department at UC and by default I studied with George Cress who taught painting and drawing. Cress was a non-figurative painter who was, and is, an artist of considerable note in the southeast. He took away my crowquills and my tiny brushes and put a number 24 hog bristle brush in my hand. He pushed me to abandon detail and to paint large, colorful abstractions in bold and broad strokes.

It was fortunate for me that he did. Otherwise the picturesque imperative might have won the day, and I might not have developed any further. But color and form and the grand scale waxed victorious in this early skirmish for my artistic soul, and I began to understand the eternal verity of Clive Bell's dictum that subject matter in art may or may not be harmful, but it is always irrelevant. This was my first epiphany, my first truly important lesson, the one that has had an everlasting effect on me and my work. I was twenty years old.

Then I became interested in printmaking.

While I was at Auburn I came across an article by a man I had never heard of: Leonard Baskin. The article was prefaced with one of the most striking images I had ever seen—a black and white figure of a man, head distorted and upturned as if in agony, rendered in lines like the veins of an onion skin. The caption said that it was a wood engraving entitled *The Death of the Laureate*.

From that day I followed Baskin's career. During the fifties and sixties, he was arguably the most profound and intellectual artist working in America. Leonard certainly would have. He was in his thirties and forties back then and was one of those rare artists who had reached a full maturity early in his life. And I was smitten by his work.

George Cress was also an admirer of Baskin's work and when he found out that I was, he encouraged me to study him.

I wanted to do a wood engraving like *The Death of the Laureate*, but there were no printmaking courses at UC. All I could learn about wood engraving was what I could find in books. And being an incompetent scholar, I found little information that shed any light on the subject. I learned only that wood engraving is done on the end grain of wood as opposed to the plank. Hardly enough information to set about learning a demanding craft. It seems a farce now, but I went to a lumber yard and bought the biggest piece of wood I could find—a six inch section of a redwood four by four. I took it home and cut into the end grain with an X-acto knife, which, as I would learn later on, was not exactly what the medium is about.

I did persist, however, and eventually mastered (or nearly mastered) the medium. As I tell my students, persistence is really what this business is all about. It has little to do with talent. Talent's about as valuable as tits on a boar. What is valuable is persistence, determination, drive, desire, patience, indefatigable energy, the willingness to fail, and luck. *Never* underestimate luck, I tell them. I've been teaching for thirty-six years now, and I've never met a student who didn't have talent. By the same token I can count on one hand the ones who manifest all the qualities I've just listed—and I'd have some fingers left over.

I persisted. And I was lucky. I left Chattanooga in 1962 and moved to New England to teach in Easthampton, Massachusetts. That's where the luck came in.

Baskin lived in the next town over, Northampton. He taught at Smith College. I knew this, of course. I remember looking up his name in the phone book and getting a rush just seeing it in such a common (and to me, personal) place. It was almost like meeting the man, although actually meeting him seemed a pipe dream. I didn't think it was possible that a Tennessee clod-hopper like me could ever meet such a world-famous artist.

But that was before I met Louis Smith.

Smitty.

Smitty was the proprietor of Smith Glass and Mirror Shop, a framing and glazing shop, and art supply store in Northampton. He was a gruff, gregarious, and generous man, who, as it turned out, was also a close friend of Baskin's. One day I took some of my drawings to Smitty's shop for him to look at. Smitty was a connoisseur of the graphic arts, and I accepted his invitation to bring in the drawings, figuring I could get some advice and criticism, and, who knows, maybe even make a sale since he was also a great collector. He looked at my drawings—owls, cocks, grotesque figures—and said, "You're pretty good, son, but you need some coaching. Who do you want to study with?"

I thought I should say Ed Hill (who was the head of the art department at Smith at the time and the author of *The Language of Drawing*), or Jack Coughlin (whose prints I had become familiar with while still in Chattanooga and who taught at the University of Massachusetts). They seemed accessible, though I knew neither one of them at the time. But then I blurted out the truth. I said, "Baskin … of course."

Smitty said, "Well, I can arrange that. Let's go."

We went out the back of the shop, got into his car, and drove over to Baskin's Fort Hill studio. We walked in unannounced. My heart was racing. What would I say to such a great artist? To God, as it were? He was at work with mallet and chisel carving a large wooden sculpture in his series of *Dead Men*. Bach was in the air—as were dust motes and wood chips. I was surprised how dark it was in the barn-like building. Baskin seemed irritated at the interruption, and after Smitty told him what we were there for, he asked me, not looking up from his work, what it was that I wanted to study.

I said, "Drawing."

He mumbled and grumbled and finally agreed, less than enthusiastically, saying that I could come by his printmaking studio at Smith the following week—if I wanted to—and we would set up a plan of some sort.

Next week, when I arrived for our appointment, he was trying to unscrew the cap of a can of liquid etching ground but couldn't get it off. He handed it to me and said, "You look like a strong lad, see if you can get this damned thing off."

I said, "It's no use, Mr. Baskin. I can't do it."

He said, "Why?"

I said, "My hands are sweating too much."

He said, "Why?"

I laughed, and said "Because I am in the same room with you."

"Nonsense, my boy," he said.

The cap stayed on the can.

As for my drawing studies, he asked me if I had something around home that I was particularly attached to. I said, "No, only my family."

He said, "Then go draw a tree. From life—no photographs! Get the smallest pen point you can find and a rough sheet of paper and do a drawing so detailed I can see every goddamned thing on it."

I left the studio full of joy that day, thinking that I had come full circle. But I hadn't.

No.

It was the beginning of a new cycle, not the culmination of an old one.

All in all I had no more than six meetings with him over the next three or four months. Each time I took a drawing of a tree for him to criticize—drawings done according to his instructions with the smallest pen nib I could find and on the best handmade drawing paper I could afford. The lessons were terse and remarkably brief. The first lesson was especially memorable: he looked at my drawing, paused ever so briefly, and dismissed it with a wave of his hand and said, "Why the hell did you do such a small drawing on such a big piece of paper?"

I said, "I don't know, sir. That's exactly the sort of thing I criticize in my students' work."

He said, "Well, go do it again."

That was that.

I left and did it again.

And again. And again. And again. And again.

And from those six meetings came three great and important lessons:

One. You must do the work over and over until it's right. Until it is better than it was before. You have to destroy the bad ones and start again. Creation only follows destruction.

Two. You must use the best materials you can possibly afford even if it means taking out a second mortgage on the house or borrowing from kin. But owning and using good materials is not enough in and of itself. You must also know and understand the nature, history, and composition of those materials. I have never made an image since with anything other than the very best materials I can afford.

And three. You must strive first to be a craftsman—to know how to put materials together into a unit—a beautiful, seamless, and coherent unit that possesses an inherent sense of inevitability and has qualities of permanence that will outlast you and, who knows, may even insure your own immortality.

Baskin's influence was powerful. It went beyond materials, craftsmanship, and composition. Indeed, it spilled over into language and took root in a new-found intellectual life—something I had always wanted but felt incapable of since I didn't read much and since all through military school I was told, repeatedly, to keep my mouth shut and let people think I was a fool rather than open it and remove all doubt.

And as I became comfortable with the fact of Baskin's humanness (plate 1), comfortable with the fact that he sat on the crapper every morning just like I do, I began to think for myself and to form and respect my own opinions, independent of his—or anyone else's.

Outside my drawing lessons with him, I had been pursuing wood engraving. Now understand that Leonard Baskin may very well be the finest wood engraver to ever pick up a graver and I never asked him to teach me anything about it. That was in part because I was afraid of him and so grateful for the other little crumbs around his table that I did not want to push my luck by being over-bearing in my requests for further elucidation.

So I went at it alone.

My wife, Kay, bought me some real engraving blocks and real engraving tools for my 27th birthday. She bought them from Smitty, and I butchered them in short order, making wood engravings that looked more like linoleum cuts or potato prints than engravings. I pulled some proofs by hand and took them for Smitty to see. He looked at them and said that he couldn't tell anything about the prints because they were so poorly printed. He said that I should take them down to Baskin's shop, The Gehenna Press, and have Harold McGrath print them for me. And I did.

It was a dreary November day and the afternoon light was failing as I walked into the shop. There was a din coming from the big Kelly 2 printing press—kind of a burly, rhythmical, chitty-chitty-bang-bang noise. The smell of machine oil, solvents, and ink was in the air. Oriental carpets on the floor and antique tables piled with books. Bookcases full of books. Books like I had never seen before. Large ones and small ones. Some in full leather bindings, some in half and quarter, though at the time I did not have those terms in my vocabulary. It was as if I had stepped into another era.

And indeed I had.

But not into the past as it seemed to me that day. No. I had stepped into the future. My future. That moment was the great epiphany in my life, and I wish I knew the exact date. It was a day for me like the day must have been for Saul of Tarsus when the scales of blindness fell from his eyes and the spirit of Jesus told him that his name, from that day forward, was Paul (which, interestingly enough, means "the runt"). I had, that day—unknown and unexpectedly—come home. Come home to my future life and to my artistic form: The Book.

It indeed was the beginning of a new life and I, like St. Paul, was indeed a runt. A dandiprat. A dapperling. A larva. And I began to weave myself a cocoon—not so much with the help of Baskin but with the help of Harold McGrath, who was at that time the finest letterpress printer in America, and who was teaching other youngsters as well, people like Lance Hidy, David Godine, and Steven Hannock.

McGrath knew of a print shop that was for sale and asked me if I would be interested in buying it. I had no money or space for such a thing so I convinced the headmaster at Williston Academy that my art department needed a printing shop. It consisted of an 18 x 24 Chandler Price clamshell press; a bank of type (mostly Goudy Oldstyle); and all the other paraphernalia that goes with a job shop. We also acquired an eighteen-inch Sturges etching press. I taught myself all I could about type and typesetting, about the presses and printing, about mordants and retroussage—quoins and nonpareils, and went to McGrath for help when utterly confounded. I read everything I could find about typography, fine printing, and limited edition books. I came under the influence of the great men of printing—Bruce Rogers, William Morris, Emery Walker, Thomas James Cobden-Sanderson, Eric Gill. I am not yet free from those influences and probably never will be, and that's all right. Typography and book design are conservative art forms that resist innovation. And since innovation usually calls attention to itself, it shows. And typography and design shouldn't show. As Eric Gill said, these arts—properly and well-practiced—are invisible arts.

And in doing all this I began finally to read, really read. As the pre-eminent American printer, the late Harry Duncan, said to me one time "setting type is the most intense form of reading there is—upside down and backwards."

And all the while I continued to butcher nice wood engraving blocks. In 1970 I was fortunate to come under the guidance of Fred Becker. He was teaching at the University of Massachusetts where I was doing graduate work. I was about to give up on engraving but he gently encouraged me not to. He told me that it was indeed a bear of a medium, but that if I persisted I would eventually get it. And I did. After two years of trying and failing, trying and failing, I finally broke through — with a print called *Icarus Agonistes* (plate 2). I knew what wood engravings were supposed to look like—I had studied plenty of them—but the muscles in my hands and arms didn't know or understand what the movements and actions were supposed to feel like. That's what took two years. Over the next eight years I polished and honed my craft—the most demanding medium there is other than, perhaps, fresco and mezzotint.

And then came children's books.

Bonnie Verberg, who was then an editor at Harcourt Brace, Jovanovich, approached me about doing a collection of six of the Br'er Rabbit stories that had been retold by the composer Van Dyke Parks. I was not very excited about it because I was faithful to the Joel Chandler Harris tellings—the ones I loved as a child and read to my own children—and because, as I complained to a close friend, I wasn't sure if I wanted to get into doing children's books.

"When it comes time to do my Bible," I said in 1984, "I don't want anyone to say that it was illustrated by a children's book illustrator."

Both those reservations were prejudiced and both proved to be illfounded. Parks' retellings were masterful, and my attitude about illustrating children's books was about to change. If it were not for having done the sixty (or so) children's books I've done in the last thirteen years, I would now be ill-prepared to do the massive work I embarked upon three years ago.

Bonnie's proposal to do *Jump!* came at an opportune time. Good engraving blocks had become scarce, and I had burned myself out doing—in a five year period—limited editions of *Alice's Adventures in Wonderland*, *Through the Looking-glass and What Alice found there*, *Adventures of Huckleberry Finn*, *Frankenstein*, and *The Wonderful Wizard of Oz*. Five big books with a total of nearly six hundred wood engravings. Five big, expensive, complicated, limited edition books for which I was not only designer and illustrator but CEO, publisher, procurer, production manager, art director, janitor, and editor-in-chief as well. And they damned near put me into Chapter Eleven. Children's books not only pulled me back from the brink of bankruptcy, they taught me a very important lesson, one that Baskin did not (and perhaps could not) teach me: how to tell a story with pictures.

And then I came back to the Bible. And with that came the great confluence of all these old and disparate facets of my life

As I see it now, all these facets taught me what I needed to know to engage the Holy Bible as an artist. I did not engage it as the inerrant and infallible word of God as did the fundamentalist preacher I once was. Rather, I engaged it as sacred literature, read and respected by an ordinary man, a profane man, an apostate. An apostate no longer moved by biblical dogma. No longer moved by biblical interpretations invented by other men struggling to imagine God and to divine His will and thus to "know" it and knowing it to call themselves His chosen. No longer moved by the homilies of men who believe they understand "the word of God" and thus interpret it to suit their own biases, purposes, and agendas.

I am, however, profoundly moved by the sometimes small and sometimes grand religious predilections of ordinary men and women (perhaps apostates as well) who have raised their flawed and uncertain voices to God. Raised them in the form of painting, and architecture, and sculpture, and books, and prints, and reliquaries, and all sorts of other things, but most of all in the form of music. It seems to me that the more the human element enters into the engagement, the closer to God the art itself becomes. I sense this in the development of liturgical music from medieval chant and song into baroque chansons and motets, becoming in time richer, showier, and filled with greater invention. In short, filled with greater humanness. I see it as small children putting on a play or dancing for the grownups gleefully squealing "Look what I can do, daddy!" I hear the voices of everyday people—if one may say that artists and craftsmen are everyday people (and I think I can, speaking as one of them)—asking to be watched, and therein lifting their voices and their stones and their gravers in celebration of that which they sense—perhaps know in a way that prelates, priests, and preachers could only hope to know—is higher and mightier than they are. Lifting voice and stone and graver in praise of that something beyond themselves which, whether they hold to any religious principles or not, breathes life into their very nostrils. Life into their stone and concrete. Life into their music and their voices. Life into their paint and clay. And, pray God, breathes life into their gravers and their illustrations for new Bibles.

LEPER & A WITCH'S GARDEN

The Beginnings of Pennyroyal Press

AFTER I CONVINCED Phillips Stevens, the headmaster at Williston Academy, that the school could no longer exist without a printing press, I looked into acquiring one. Harold McGrath knew of an old 18 x 24 Chandler Price and a couple of cabinets of mostly old and worn-out types that were for sale. It belonged to Fred Rau, a printer who worked at Metcalf Printing, located next door to Leonard Baskin's Gehenna Press on Clark Avenue in Northampton. I persuaded Mr. Stevens to buy it, and in the late spring of 1969, we moved Rau's entire print shop from Turner's Falls, Massachusetts, to its new home in Easthampton.

The press was bolted to the floor of a room in the old Easthampton Railway Station, which at one time had been the Railway Express Office. The building had been acquired by Williston some years earlier and was at that time being used as a repair shop for school furniture and for storage of snow removal equipment. In the summer we bought a proof press from a newspaper in North Adams, Massachusetts, that was phasing out its hot metal typesetting. When we hauled that monster off the truck and put it on the floor of the shop, I had all the printing equipment I would have for the next six years.

My students and I called the fledgling operation The Castalia Press. It was 1969 and the drug culture was growing, as were the reputations of Timothy Leary and the Baba Ram Dass (who, as Richard Alpert, was a Williston alumnus, and from whose father the railroad station was originally purchased). Castalia, the name of the mythological spring on Mount Parnassus, was the name of Leary's foundation in Millbrook, New York. The connections, at that time, just seemed "too cool" to pass up.

The first printed piece was an announcement of the establishment of the Press, stating that our purpose was to be printers of "belles-lettres," mostly because we wanted to avoid the inevitable requests to print football schedules, grade forms, and dance invitations.

Since Williston Academy was a non-profit institution, a fiscal dilemma soon arose regarding my making books and prints which I intended to sell for my own profit. Wilmot Babcock, Williston's business manager, suggested that I produce my work under another press name.

So, "Pennyroyal" came to be.

The choice of the name was, first of all, influenced by Mandragora Press, the name David Godine was then using for his limited edition work. Mandragora is the genus name of the mandrake, a plant, as legend holds, that grows at the foot of scaffolds nurtured by the hanged man's blood, and screams when plucked from the earth. My then-current fascination with witchcraft, demonology, and plant lore seemed to be a fertile place to look for a name. Pennyroyal, I learned from Dorothy Jacob's book *A Witch's Guide to Gardening*, is "a plant common to every witch's garland." As a word, Pennyroyal seemed an interesting oxymoron, if nothing else, because it played on my wanting to do grand and regal books though I had no money. I wish now that I had been less self-conscious and precious about the naming of the press and had simply called it The Moser Press. Today the historic allusion to Thomas Bird Mosher's The Mosher Press is more interesting to me than the herbal, witchcraft allusion. Alas, hindsight.

I began reading everything I could find on the history of private presses, the history of the book, book design, paper making, binding, lettering, calligraphy, and typography: Paul Bennett, Douglas McMurtrie, Graily Hewitt, Eric Gill, Dard Hunter, Douglas Cockerell, Roderick Cave, Alfred Fairbank, Colin Clair, Emil Ruder, D. B. Updike, Rudolph Koch, Alexander Nesbitt, John Howard Benson, Oscar Ogg, Paul Standard, Stanley Morison, Edward Johnston, Herman Degering, Frederic Goudy, Egon Weiss, Adrian Wilson, Hugh Williamson. From the beginning, I aimed to produce books in the true idiosyncratic spirit of the private press, which to me meant making books which would reflect the tastes, interests, and passions of one person—its proprietor, me. From 1970 to 1974 I produced six books under the Pennyroyal imprint and two books under the Castalia imprint, including my first book, a slender and unevenly printed presentation of an essay by James Abbott McNeill Whistler called "The Red Rag," from his book *The Gentle Art of Making Enemies*.

I hand set the type, 18-point Goudy Oldstyle, and printed it on the Chandler Price using a lovely Italian paper called Amalfi. I didn't know any binders at that time, so I took the finished and folded signatures to a commercial binder in South Hadley Falls, Massachusetts who bound the edition of fifty copies in a stiff quarter leather binding. The title page faced a frontispiece portrait of Mr. Whistler that I would have liked to have been my first "published" engraving. I had been living with Baskin's little wood engraving called *The Leper* for a few years by that time, studying it and admiring it on a daily basis. And I had been trying, with little success, to get a handle on that devilish medium by emulating Baskin's style. What seems now a simple job was then frightening and out of the question since the four or five engravings I had done up to that point looked more like linoleum cuts than engravings. So out of the necessity born of inability I stooped to making a scratch board portrait of Whistler, and from that had a photographic line cut made from which the frontispiece was printed.

Etching was, for me, then, an easier medium to handle than wood engraving, so the next project I did was a portfolio of etchings on what I called a "Botanico-Erotic" theme. It was called *The Death of the Narcissus*, and consisted of eleven sequential images, a haiku poem by Onitsura printed in 48-point Centaur, a title page, half title, and colophon. It was laid into a rather ill-fitting tray case that was, again, made by the South Hadley Book Bindery.

I was teaching my students at Williston as I was teaching myself—teaching classes in typography, printmaking, printing, design, and life drawing. But I wanted to learn more than I was able to teach myself, so I applied to the MFA program at the University of Massachusetts in Amherst. I had met Jack Coughlin a couple of years before and was confident that I could get into the program and would be able to do the work, despite the fact that I had been turned down for graduate studies previously at the University of Denver and the University of Georgia.

I was accepted in 1970 and went to classes at night and did independent studies on my own, one of which was with Fred Becker, who taught relief printmaking. Fred, a master wood engraver in his own right, encouraged me not to give up on engraving wood, something I was very much tempted to do at that point.

He gently nudged me into doing an illustrated book as my independent study with him, hand setting the type and illustrating it with wood engravings. I took the challenge and the result was another slender volume called *Bacchanalia*: ten wood engravings with six epigrams from the *Anthologia Græca* that were translated by my friend Douglas Graham who was teaching at Williston at the time (plate 3). It was a seminal work for me and for Pennyroyal Press because it forced me to confront wood engraving on a daily basis, and forced the muscles of my head and hand to memorize all the moves. The engravings were inconsistent, but, by God, they actually looked like wood engravings. They even bore a faint resemblance to *The Leper*.

After that I continued to make slender books, broadsides, pamphlets, and small portfolios, working at night, weekends, vacations, and in between classes. One of those portfolios was a second treatment of the myth of Narcissus. Flipping the usual rôles of author and illustrator I called upon another friend, the poet E. M. Beekman, to write a poem for a sequence of wood cuts which were on a botanical, auto-erotic theme similar to *The Death of the Narcissus*. The new *Narcissus* was finished in 1974. It was printed on handmade Italia and was laid in a box that was made by David Bourbeau, Carolyn Coman, and Barbara Blumenthal.

In 1974, my friend Gordon Cronin introduced me to Jeffrey Dwyer. The two of them had just opened Dwyer & Cronin, Booksellers, a used bookstore in Amherst, Massachusetts. Dwyer and I hit it off immediately and (with Cronin and John Nelson, a professor at the University of Massachusetts, as editor) we produced *Twelve American Writers*. It was Pennyroyal's first collaboration.

In 1975 I was hurting for money and hungry to expand the scope and scale of my books. I approached a group of people who had been collecting my work for a period of years and sold each of them a "patronship" in Pennyroyal for five hundred dollars. As a benefit of their patronship, they would receive all future Pennyroyal Press publications at a significant discount. With this money, I produced *Men of Printing*, edited by Jack Walsdorf (plate 4), and E. M. Beekman's *Carnal Lent*.

I hired Rich Hendel to design these books because I felt that they were too important for me to use as exercises for my still developing design skills. Rich Hendel was at that time the design and production manager at the University of Massachusetts Press. It was he who had given me my very first book work: a drawing for the dust jacket of Ely Green's autobiography *Ely: Too Black, Too White*. He had also commissioned me to do four hundred drawings for Vernon Ahmadjian's *The Flowering Plants of Massachusetts*, which, as it turned out, was highly influential on the early Pennyroyal books, which were replete with botanical themes.

McGrath printed *Men of Printing* and *Carnal Lent* under the pseudonym "Harold Patrick" at the Gehenna Press. These were the only two books he printed for me under that *nom de plume*. Annie O'Connor, one of my best students at what had by this time become The Williston Academy–Northampton School for Girls was Pennyroyal's first apprentice after she graduated in 1975. She set the type for *Carnal Lent*, and worked on several other projects, including the Arion Press *Moby-Dick* and the Abattoir Editions presentation of Paul Smyth's *Thistles and Thorns* that was printed by Harry Duncan.

In 1976, Leonard Baskin took his Gehenna Press to England, and set up a new shop in Devon. The ownership of the old printing equipment was transferred to McGrath. That same year, Dwyer, McGrath, and I, along with John Locke, Ruth Mortimer and John Lancaster, founded a letterpress printing company. We called it the Hampshire Typothetæ and set it up in a building on Market Street in Northampton which was previously an Irish tavern called "Brendan's." The place had huge holes in the floor, reeked of stale beer and urine, and needed a lot of work. So we tore the place apart and rebuilt it. The renovations were completed on April 4, 1977. We moved all the equipment from Clark Avenue to Market Street and once again began to produce books. We were in that location until 1981, during which time Chase Twichell, Jane Lancaster, Michael Secondo, Carolyn Hartwell, Betse Curtis, and Arthur Larson helped me produce some of Pennyroyal's best work.

In the summer of 1979, Pennyroyal acquired a small Colts Armory Press and some more type from Father William Fletcher. The equipment had belonged to the Red Coat Press, and God only knows how Father Fletcher came into possession of it. Nevertheless, Dwyer, McGrath, Lancaster and I drove to Southport, Connecticut in a rented sixteen-wheel rig to haul it back to Market Street. It was a hot day in July. The equipment and type were more voluminous than we were anticipating and we were expected to take every rigelet, lead, and copper. By the time we had it all packed up and lagged to the truck bed it was mid-afternoon. Coming home on I-91 one of the tires blew out and we had to pull off and wait for assistance from the rental company. We waited in a service station watching Spencer Tracy and Frederic March in *Inherit the Wind*. By the time we got to Northampton it was too late to return the truck to the rental agency so we drove it over to MacGrath's house and parked it overnight in his backyard. Then we all met at our usual watering hole, Joe's Cafe, a bar and pizza joint across the street from our shop. We were so dehydrated from heat, sun, and sweat that we drank several pitchers of beer without one of us ever getting up to take a leak. By the time we left we were all knee-walking drunk. Dwyer went into the Typothetæ to use the head and locked the door after him. McGrath was following Dwyer and as he was trying to unlock the door, Dwyer lifted the lid of the mail slot in the door, stuck his business through it, and pissed on the "old man." When McGrath finally did manage to get the door open he charged in. The next thing I saw was Dwyer running out the back door of the building with McGrath in hot pursuit, yelling and shaking his fist. The last I saw of them they were running down Market Street, Mac yelling, Dwyer falling and rolling and laughing and getting up and running again. Mac chased him as well as he could in his drunken state, hollering and cussing all the while. They disappeared around the corner at Main Street. I was content to piss on a fire hydrant.

In 1976 I met Paul Mariani. He came to me at the suggestion of Jack Coughlin to have a book of his poems printed and possibly illustrated. He had been a student of Allen Mandelbaum of whom I had done a portrait for David Godine's edition of Mandelbaum's *Chelmaxioms*. Mandelbaum was going to underwrite part of the costs. When I read the manuscript of *Timing Devices* I called Mariani and told him that I would not only do the book but that I would absorb whatever costs Mandelbaum did not cover. Paul has been a friend ever since and as scholar, poet, and editor has contributed much to the development of Pennyroyal Press. *Timing Devices* was the first Pennyroyal book to be released as a trade book. It was published by David Godine.

In 1980, faced with the mortgage payment for the Market Street shop and the combined rents of my studio and apartment in Northampton, I sought to consolidate expenses by finding a location where all the activities of studio and printing shop would be under one roof. Harold and I went to West Hatfield, Massachusetts, to look at a house that was for sale that had a large adjacent garage. It was only four miles from Market Street. We figured that the garage, with a small addition and some minor renovations, would be perfect for our shop, and that the house was more than sufficient to fulfill my needs for home and studio. The renovations were completed in 1981 and the equipment was moved from Market Street. It was almost more than the old Kelly 2 could take, but it made the trip like a trouper. It was at this shop that we accomplished the major work of Pennyroyal Press: *Alice's Adventures in Wonderland*, *Through the Looking-Glass and what Alice found there*, *Frankenstein*, *Adventures of Huckleberry Finn*, and *The Wonderful Wizard of Oz*.

As the supplies of good wood engraving blocks dwindled and the stings of having been nearly bankrupted by the poor sales of all but *Alice's Adventures in Wonderland*, my enthusiasm for doing books in the grand manner waned. It was sparked into life again in 1986 when I met Eudora Welty and we decided to do a new edition of her *The Robber Bridegroom* that was published the following year. Two years after that, Pennyroyal Press published Norman Maclean's *A River Runs Through It*. Dwyer had read the book years before and thought that it would be successful if properly presented. I wrote to the University of Chicago press and suggested a collaborative effort to bring the book out in a fine press edition, with each press sharing some of the financial responsibilities. The idea was met warmly, but I was told that it could not happen without Mr. Maclean's approval. So I wrote to him. I did not spell out any of my ideas, I just sought his permission. He called me one day and asked me what I intended to do with it, adding very sternly that he didn't want anybody "fucking with" his family. I told him that my idea was to do small illustrations of some of George Croonenburghs' trout flies and to punctuate them at every fourth "beat" by larger images of a can of worms, his brother's fishing hat, a portrait of his brother, and a portrait of George himself. He was very much taken with the idea of the fourth beat since it was a direct extrapolation of his dictum that fly fishing is an art "that is performed on a four-count rhythm between ten and two o'clock."

So I took that four-count rhythm and went with it. We produced the Pennyroyal Press edition of *A River Runs Through It* in 1989. I felt then, with the scarcity of good engraving blocks becoming more and more severe, and with McGrath's growing forgetfulness, that we had surely produced the last Pennyroyal book. Though, with Maclean, I hoped that one day another fish, one larger perhaps than all those that had come before, might arise in the Arctic half-light of my canyon.

ished and shiny. And they have a sleigh. A big red sleigh with removable side boards painted a deep pine-needle green with red and white pin-stripes that intersect at the top corners in elaborately detailed arabesques.

Last February, a few days after the blizzard that hit on the 8th and dumped snow on us for two solid days, I drove up to visit the babies and grandbabies and have dinner with them. My son-in-law, Dan, owns a delicatessen and is a pretty good cook. The roads were clear by early afternoon, as was the sky, which was a blinding Bonnie blue. I drove my SAAB, leaving my 4-wheel drive Jeep at home.

Just as the sun was going down and the first cocktails were being mixed, David Sienkowski knocked on the back door and invited us all to go for a sleigh ride. Cara declined because Izzy, the oldest grandbaby, was running at the nose and the littlest baby, Eliza, was asleep—a rare moment. Dan was about to go, but Cara reminded him that he promised to fix dinner and had better be about it, so he declined too. Me? Hell, I poured myself a stout snort of bourbon whiskey in a small mason jar, put on my Land's End down parka, pulled my cap down around my ears, and went along. David, me, Percy and Otis, and Jimmy Beam.

We stopped at the intersection of Main Street and Route 9 to make sure no traffic was coming—then a "Giddy-up," a slap of the reins, and away we went, the bells on Otis and Percy's harnesses raising a ruckus and the sleigh scraping across the nearly bare pavement. Once we were on the other side of the highway we took off into the woods, heading towards the fairgrounds.

Now that we were in deep snow it was quiet enough to carry on a conversation, which we tried to do, but soon found that we really didn't have all that much to talk about. We descended into small talk with David doing most of the talking—gossip and anecdotes and real estate information about Cummington and its residents. He pointed out that the land we were on was for sale. Said it belonged to one Mr. James L. Kurtz. Well, I know Jimmy Kurtz. He is an irascible sort of guy who owns a used car lot over in Northampton. I like him, despite his manners. He lives in Goshen, a wide spot of a village that sits between Northampton and Cummington. I knew that Jimmy owned property in Cummington, but had no idea where it was in relationship to my daughter's house. And—I thought to myself—it was a good thing he didn't know we were on his land. Knowing him, he'd be liable to get royally pissed off. He's peculiar that way.

And then … wouldn't you know … it started in snowing again. At that moment I wished I had been with a lady friend instead of David because it was so beautiful and romantic, especially when we came out of the woods and stopped at the edge of a frozen lake—I think they call it Shumway Pond. David thought that was right too, but he didn't know for sure either. He said a lot of people call it by a lot of names. Later on I looked for it on a map but I couldn't find it. Well, I tell you—that was a beautiful sight sitting there between that pond and those woods watching the snow come down. And we could see, believe it or not. Even in that real flat winter dark we could see. The snow seemed to give off its own light. It seemed iridescent, almost. We could even see the horses' breath in the frozen air. There was a light, a single light, way off in the distance, coming from a farmhouse on the side of a hill. David told me that was the McKenna farm. They raised Holsteins.

We stayed there for a few minutes. It was that wonderful snow quiet— you all know what I'm talking about. The only thing we could hear was the horses breathing and an occasional jangle of a harness bell. And there I was, an old southern boy wrapped up in goose down, sittin' in a fine looking, hand-painted horse-drawn New England sleigh, listening to those harness bells a-jinglin' and watching that distant farmhouse light twinkle through the downfall of snow which was gathering in my beard and melting on my cheeks and glasses. But despite the picture-postcard beauty of the scene, I was gettin' cold—real cold. But, of course, being a male of our species, I wouldn't have admitted it for anything in the world. Wouldn't have wanted young Sienkowski there to think I was a middle-aged wimp or anything like that, so I said, "Hey, David, reckon we can turn this rig around and go back? We been gone for a while now, and I did promise the kids I'd have supper with them. Dan's probably already got it on the table and it's getting cold. And besides, I'm gettin' a little worried about this snow—I didn't drive my 4-wheel and I've got a long drive home."

A long drive home.

A long drive home? What have I just done?

I've just told you a whole bunch of lies is what I've done. A bunch of fancy and frivolous lies woven in and around a few facts: my daughter and her family do live in Cummington, as do Richard and Charly Wilbur. Cara's neighbors names are Sharon and Bob Cunningham, and so far as I know they own neither horse nor sleigh. I have ridden on a sleigh like the one I described—around a short one-mile circle at the Swift River Inn, which is in Plainfield, not Cummington, with Cara, her babies, and Dan who was at that time one of the managers of the Inn. It was a sunny Sunday morning. There is no Jimmy Kurtz that I know of. No Shumway Pond either—certainly couldn't find it on a map. I made it up. I made all of it up. None of it is true. Or is it?

What I did, obviously, was to paraphrase Robert Frost's well-known poem "Stopping by Woods on a Snowy Evening." I told you essentially the same story, but intentionally drowned it in a sea of details to make it convincing and to hide what I was doing. I told you a great deal more than Mr. Frost did—the horses' names, the color of the sleigh, details of its paint job, who owned the woods, why I was out there, all sorts of anecdotal decorations. And that's precisely what's wrong with it. It's picturesque. Its emphasis is on detail and variety rather than on form and unity. I told too much. I did not ask anything of you but that you listen and be entertained and comforted. This is not art.

You will not remember my little story. Oh, I know some of you may remember one or two details from it. Some of you may remember more, but you will forget who told you. Or where. Such is the nature of entertainment.

But, how many of you will forget Mr. Frost's poem? None. That is because Frost's poem is not story. It's rhythms. It's words—memorable words.

Robert Francis has a poem, "Poppycock," which bears witness to this point. It goes like this:

> *Could be a game*
> *like battledore*
> *and shuttlecock.*
> *Could be.*

Could be a color
red
but none of your commie red
damn you!

Red of a cocky cock's
cockscomb
or scarlet poppies
popping in a field of wheat.

But poppycock
after all
alas is only
poppycock.

In other words bilge
bosh
buncombe
baloney

ballyhoo from Madison A
ballyhoo from Washington DC
red-white-and-blue poppycock.
Hurrah!

There are other cocks
to be sure.
Petcocks
weathercocks

barnyard cocks
bedroom cocks
cocksure
or cockunsure.

But to get back to poppycock
what a word!
God! What a word!
Just the word!

Keep your damn poems
only give me the words
they are made of.
Poppycock!

At the core of all good art is design and craftsmanship. Mr. Frost's design and craftsmanship made memorable art out of what would otherwise have been merely an ephemeral anecdote like mine.

Maybe Mr. Frost was out on a snowy evening. Maybe he was alone. Maybe he did pass by a stand of woods that belonged to somebody he knew who lived in Ripton, or Goshen Corners, or Bread Loaf.

Then again, maybe the event never happened. Maybe, like my story, it is a lie. But that is no matter to the art form, to the poetry or the fiction, because although art may be a "lie" in terms of realistic representation, it is a truth unto itself. Whether he stopped by those woods or not makes no difference whatsoever. What does make a difference is that a line of a poem came into his head—who knows which line it was? Or how fully formed it was. Perhaps it was merely a question he asked himself or a companion, "I wonder whose woods these are...?" Or perhaps he thought to himself "Damn, I can't just sit here all night watching this snowfall, I got promises to keep..." Whatever the line, whatever the words, we can be sure that they came in a pattern, a rhythm. We can be sure that they were musical, and they sparked something beyond themselves which would otherwise have remained formless and anecdotal until Frost welded them into a poem.

Many writers emphasize this. In her essay, "Place in Fiction," Eudora Welty says that all fiction is a lie because it's written to serve its own purposes, and not to apply to anything outside itself. If that makes it "fancy and frivolous," as she calls it, so be it. Because artful words, like those of Mr. Frost's poem, are really the rhythmic dance of sounds across the page or off the lips.

In fact, art always works best when the personal connection—the reality connection—is broken, so that the details, the anecdotes, wear what Nancy Willard calls "the livery of art," not the livery of representation.

Clive Bell, in his 1914 aesthetic treatise *Art*, laid the foundation for this kind of 20th century art criticism when he said that the "representational element in a work of art may or may not be harmful, but it is always irrelevant. For to appreciate a work of art, we must bring with us nothing from life, no knowledge of its affairs and ideas, no familiarity with its emotions." I was for a long while a staunch adherent and promulgator of this philosophy, but now, I would it amend it a little bit. Soften its stance on the irrelevance of the representational aspect of art. It's more apt, I think, to say that we *need not* bring anything with us from life when we appreciate a work of art. Because all art that ignores the humanness of its very nature is empty, vapid, and worthless except as a curiosity of history. So, as appreciators, we walk a fine line, reveling in sound design and impeccable craftsmanship, while allowing the human aspects to speak to our soul.

It is the same with making good pictures or good books.

The very first book I did (in 1970) was an essay by James Abbot McNeil Whistler, the author of a very famous picture of his mother that practically everybody knows as *Whistler's Mother*, which isn't the title of the picture. The real title, *Arrangement in and Gray and Black*, says a great deal about the painting and about the author's intentions. Let me read you a few of Mr. Whistler's own words:

"Art should be independent of all clap-trap—should stand alone, and appeal to the artistic sense of eye or ear, without confounding this with emotions entirely foreign to it, [like] devotion, pity, love, patriotism, and the like. All these have no kind of concern with it, and that is why I insist on calling my works 'arrangements' and 'harmonies.'

"Take the picture of my mother, exhibited at the Royal Academy as *An Arrangement in Grey and Black*. Now that is what it is. To me it is interesting as a picture of my mother, but what can or ought the public to care about the identity of the portrait?"

Earlier in his essay, which is entitled "The Red Rag," Whistler said that the "vast majority of English folk cannot and will not consider a picture as a picture, apart from any story which it may be supposed to tell.

"My picture of a *Harmony in Grey and Gold* is an illustration of my meaning—a snow scene with a single black figure and a lighted tavern. I care nothing," he says, "for the past, present or future of the black figure, placed there because the black was wanted at that spot. All I know is that my combination of grey and gold is the basis of the picture. Now this is precisely what my friends cannot grasp."

As a teacher with over twenty years experience in the high school classroom, I often told parents of "talented" children—talented, they thought, because the child could draw a dog or cat that looked like a dog or cat—that talent is one of the most common attributes on the face of the earth, as common as house dust. This truth prompted Herman Melville to say that nothing "is more unsuccessful than common men with talent." Or, to say it another way, nothing is more common than unsuccessful men with talent. I then tell the crestfallen and (typically) defensive parents of "talented" children that making pictures is more than making resemblances and likenesses. No matter how hard one might try, no one—no one—has ever made a drawing or a painting of a dog or cat or an anything else that was, in fact, a dog or cat or anything else. What one can make is a drawing or a painting (or in my case, a book). And it must be understood that those things are made with the elements and materials of pictures and books. Those things are line, shape, form, color, texture, rhythms, paper, canvas, paint, space, ink, type, and so on. They are not made with mothers, or snowy woods, or sleighs, or bells, or Belgian horses. You cannot—no matter how hard you try or how hard you might want to—make a dog. Joyce Kilmer might have said that fools like me make paintings, but only God can make a dog.

On the first day of my class at Rhode Island School of Design I some-times instruct my students to watch me very closely as I begin a drawing on the chalk board. I compel them to notice everything I do, even untoward scratches. They do. They don't know me well enough yet not to. They watch as a drawing of an apple, always an apple, slowly develops on the chalk board. When I "finish" I stand back, pretending to show intellectual and artistic doubt and dissatisfaction. I return to the board two or three times and put a few finishing touches to it. Then, I put my chalk on the chalk tray, dust off my hands as I turn to the class and ask with a nod to the drawing, "What is that?"

And someone always volunteers the answer.

"It's an apple."

I turn on the proud volunteer and shout (in mock rage) "Bullshit, it's an apple!" I turn to the blackboard with as much madness and rage as I can pretend, and smear the drawing of the apple into a dusty grey blur. Then I turn to my agape students, my chalky palms held outward for them to see, and say (gently) "No. It's not an apple—it's chalk isn't it? Never, ever forget that. Never forget that when you make pictures all you have to work with is your raw material and your imagination. If, 'in a most rare hour' in the course of the next thirty years or so, you have done a painting, or a draw-ing, or a poem, or a book that transcends its raw materials, and thus becomes art, you will be very fortunate. But for now, concern yourself not with art but with your materials and your craftsmanship, with seeing, and with chalk. Concern yourself with 'the livery of art.'"

Thoughts On Being an Artist

I.

It may be a point of great pride to have a Van Gogh on the living room wall, but the prospect of having Van Gogh himself in the living room would put a good many devoted art lovers to rout. —Ben Shahn

I WOULD SUPPOSE, and there is no way for me to verify this, that other than writers, poets, and morticians, the profession of artist is generally the least understood of all human endeavors. Along with male hair dressers, politicians, and auto mechanics, it is the profession most stereotyped. Artists are, in the public view, neurotic, or at least goofy; lazy, or at least lax in their bathing habits; gay, or at least peculiar in their sexual activities; prone to substance abuse, or at least alcoholic; poor, or at least undernourished dreamers.

These stereotypes exist in part, I think, because, as Ben Shahn suggests, history has given us the models: Vincent Van Gogh and Rudolph Bresdin immediately come to mind. But the stereotypes persist, I think, because the American public, at least, neither cares about nor understands how artists work. The public does not understand, for instance, that the work is, first of all, unspeakably difficult; they do not understand that the work is solitary in nature; they do not understand that the work is terrifying, because the artist so seldom knows what he's doing. And because, as someone once said, what the artist's husband doesn't understand is that when she's sitting staring out a window, she's working.

II.

I've written five books and what happens is you know less and less. Each time you realize you don't know what you thought you knew. It's terrifying. The things you know you have accomplished are invisible to you and all you are aware of are the outer edges of your culpability and the darkness out there. So you always have the sense of yourself as an absolute beginner. I think that is the place to be if you want to continue: not sitting complacently in your own light, but off where it's really scary. —E. L. Doctorow

I HAVE DONE A NUMBER OF BOOKS and have been called an artist from time to time, yet I refer to myself as an artist on only the rarest and soberest ocasions. When asked what I do for a living, I usually respond with something like, "Oh, I'm a designer," or, "I illustrate books," or, "I'm an engraver," or, "I'm a printmaker," or, "I'm a teacher." Because, you see, to me, "artist" is a title. Goya was an artist. Velásquez was an artist. Rico Lebrun was an artist. And for me to put myself in the company of artists of that caliber takes more temerity than I can usually muster. I must wait for my peers and for the refining fires of time to call me that.

So what is an artist? In my opinion, an artist is a maker of things: a picture maker, a pot maker, a poem maker. Now, pictures and poems and pots can be made—and are made—by people who are not artists—"*soi-disants*," as e.e. cummings called them, and the result of *soi-disants* making pictures and pots and poems is usually feculence (one need only to pick up a recent issue of *Art in America* to get my drift). On the other hand, pictures and pots and poems can be made—and are made—by craftsmen, and the results of craftsmen making pictures and pots and poems are good pictures and good pots and good poems, because the craftsman knows how to handle materials and tools, and because the craftsman has training and a sense of history. But his pictures and pots and poems may remain, forever, no more than good pictures and good pots and good poems.

Then there are the pictures and pots and poems made by artists, which become art. And art is what happens when the artist (a craftsman himself, a man or woman of taste and a sense of history as well as a man or woman of knowledge, culture, and daring) transcends both self and materials, and the picture or pot or poem glistens and gleams, iridescent with mystery. And the world is left rubbing its eyes and asking, "How the hell did he do that?" And the artist is left asking himself, perhaps a year or two later, "How the hell did I do that?"

III.

Excellence is the perfect excuse. Do it well and it matters little what.
—Ralph Waldo Emerson

MAKING THINGS WELL is an addiction. And to get a fix, the artist has to makes things often. Take Honoré Daumier, for instance. He worked for three or four daily newspapers making what we today think of as political cartoons. He made thousands of lithographs, day in and day out. Some are merely interesting, others are good. And then, like the brightest star in a constellation, there is the *Rue Transonia*, one of the greatest prints in the history of printmaking.

The maker of things who makes things well and makes things frequently is driven by imagination. e. e. cummings said that he was "certain of nothing but the holiness of the heart's affection and the truth of the imagination." George Bernard Shaw said that dreaming and imagination could drive an Irishman crazy because it is such a torture, and that "only whiskey makes it possible."

The artist makes things well and has little concern for originality, or fashion, or for being cool. Being, as artists must be, cultured, the artist understands that he or she is not an end product of some wonderful and mysterious process of evolution. He realizes that he is a way station, a mere moment, a moment with a foot in the past and a foot in the future, and owing a debt to both. I daresay that with a work schedule such as the one Daumier carried, he spent precious little time considering whether or not his work was "original." If one studies the history of art, one cannot help but be struck with the obvious fact that all art has antecedents.

IV.

Of making books there is no end. —*Ecclesiastes 12:12*

THERE ARE FEW PLACES LEFT in the publishing world where the book is governed more by content and form than by the dictates of the marketplace. In what is becoming a sadly homogeneous world of trade books (published with less than brilliant fiscal acumen, though with the bottom line always in mind), the small press is perhaps the last bastion of dedication to both the *art of the book*, which is to say that careful, learned, informed attention is lavished on type, paper, presswork, design, illustration, bindings, and so forth, and to *new voices* in contemporary letters, which is not to say that older, even ancient, voices are ignored by the small private press because they certainly are not.

Unlike the world of trade books there are no rules in the world of the small press. Experimentation is frequently the order of the day, along with a hefty measure of risk taking. The small press exists solely for the satisfaction of its proprietor and that proprietor's idiosyncrasies. It goes without saying that once a committee or a board of directors is established, the small press is no longer small, at least not in the way I, as a proprietor of a small press, think of small presses.

The world of the small press is not homogeneous. Given the disparities between individual tastes and opinions regarding literature, poetry, design, illustration, and political leanings, small presses yield a commensurately wide range of products: from tiny, inexpensively produced flip books to weighty, expensively produced Bibles. Some small presses produce esoteric books that break away from traditions to offer the "reader" nothing save the book itself. And sometimes the results are objects of breathtaking beauty. Most small presses, like mine, adhere to the old ways and produce books in the traditional mode using handmade papers, specially commissioned types & calligraphy, impeccable press work, and handmade bindings wrought in leather or vellum. And here again the results are sometimes objects of breathtaking beauty.

But to produce a book by hand is a frighteningly expensive process and the final price tag of "press books" represents that hard fact, a fact that sticks in my craw. Books should not be precious objects that are reserved only for the well-heeled. They should be available to anyone who wants to see and read them. They should be handled and read and stacked and shelved.

The hope (my hope, anyway) is that the costly, finely made book will find its way to a trade house that will produce a handsome and inexpensive facsimile of it, making it available to a wider audience. That done, one can then dare to hope that the design and aesthetic sensibilities of the small press will find their way into the mainstream world of the trade book because well-designed books are no more expensive to produce than poorly designed books. This is one lesson that the world of trade books could learn from the small press. That and the willingness to risk occasional economic failure by publishing things that ought to be published rather than publishing bumfodder that inevitably find its worthless way to its deserved place on the remainder table.

V.

A living failure is better than a dead masterpiece. —George Bernard Shaw

ENERGY IS A BASIC PRECONDITION for the "creative" life. Without it we would never persist in the ever-present face of failure—because we do fail. A lot. It takes a long time to realize that failing is ok. Failing, and recognizing that we have failed, is what keeps us working. Otherwise, old man Complacency sneaks in and colors the work we do with the look and smell of the ordinary and the indulgent. William Faulkner said that "failure is worth while and admirable, provided only that the failure is splendid enough, the dream splendid enough, unattainable enough yet forever valuable enough, since it was of perfection."

Energy and courage are both necessary to simply endure the grueling years that it takes to master a craft—years with little or no psychic or financial reward. Indeed, art is long and life is short, but let me tell you that it takes years of torturous trials and agonizing errors to learn how to control and manipulate physical, plastic materials—paint, wood, type, paper, words, sounds—the empirical and concrete verities that give rise to expression and form to ideas.

I think of it as grammar.

As I speak, and indeed as I write, I do not think about nor weigh my use of nouns and pronouns, verbs and adverbs, predicate nominative complements or predicate adjective complements—much less the possessive modifying gerunds. If I do, I become verbally constipated. It is likewise with visual grammar. As I paint and draw and engrave, I do not think about nor weigh my use of line and shape, rhythm and chiaroscuro, or simultaneous contrasts and split-complementary color schemes. If I do, I become visually constipated.

As my old friend E. M. Beekman says, we have to learn grammar so well that we forget it. We have to take liberties with it, and move on to more important things like making the objects we call art, all of which—by their very nature—transcend their grammar and their materials. And to endure all this takes indefatigable energy, unwavering courage—and an ardent devotion to the habit of work.

VI.

Maxima debetur puero reverentia. [The greatest respect is due to a child.]
—*Juvenal*

A BRIEF SPEECH GIVEN AT RAINBOW BABIES AND CHILDREN'S HOSPITAL IN CLEVELAND, OHIO, OCTOBER I, 1993

A FRIEND OF MINE, Douglas Graham, told me a story about a friend of his back in England who was once in the service of King George VI. When George died, Douglas' friend was charged with the responsibility of taking the news to Winston Churchill. He was to tell nobody else but Churchill. When he arrived at 10 Downing Street, he was told to go away because Mr. Churchill was writing a speech and was adamant about not being interrupted. The young man insisted, saying that he was on special order of the Queen Mother. When he was finally admitted to the Prime Minister's study, he saw Churchill leaning against the mantle of the fireplace, staring into the fire. He was clearly irritated at the interruption, so the young man quickly told Churchill the news of George's death. The Prime Minister sat down at his desk and with a broad sweep of his arm swept everything off of it, then pounded it with his fist exclaiming "Earth-shaking events happen while stupid men like me write speeches."

I know that feeling today.

Children suffer pain and are dying while stupid men like me paint and engrave pictures.

After being with these children today, and seeing the work of this hospital and the skills of its staff, my work does seem stupid. I can only hope and pray that my books may take the children's minds off their pain—even for just a moment. And I hope and pray that for a moment, an hour, or a day, my work might delight, encourage and perhaps inspire a child to make something. To shape, to invent, and to play—yes, to play, that great grandmother of all the arts! And in that rare and wonderful moment, hour, day of shaping and inventing and playing, may they soar above their trials and transcend their plight.

Caught Stealing

New England Children's Literature Festival
July 18, 1994

What has been is what will be, and what has been done is what will be done; and there is nothing new under the sun. —*Ecclesiastes*

God and posterity are only served by well-made objects. —*Flannery O'Connor*

Immature poets imitate; mature poets steal. —*T. S. Eliot*

WHEN I GRADUATED FROM HIGH SCHOOL in 1958, my parents gave me a portable high-fi for my graduation present. The first record I bought featured Mario Lanza as *The Student Prince*. I still have it. I also bought recordings by Mantovani, Percy Faith, and the Platters. I didn't care a whole lot for Elvis, but I was really keen on Johnny Mathis. My musical taste has improved over the years.

One of my favorite Johnny Mathis songs was a tune called "Many Are the Paths to One God." It was a tune that meant a lot to me back then because, you see, I had gotten myself good and saved that summer at a revival meeting at the Brainerd Methodist Church in Chattanooga and had dedicated myself to God and to the ministry of the Gospel of Jesus Christ. I became a licensed Methodist preacher on March 24, 1960. But, like my understanding of, and taste in, music, my theology has changed and matured over the years. But one thing has not changed: I still believe, like the Johnny Mathis song says, that there is no one path to God—or to whatever God is. I am not arrogant enough to say what God is. I leave that to the likes of those who can—Billy Graham, Pat Robertson, Jimmy Swaggart, Garner Ted Armstrong, Jerry Falwell. But suffice it to say that, for me and for tonight, I believe that God is the Creative Force in the universe—an Ascendancy far, far greater than anything my human mind could imagine.

What keeps me from being an atheist is that every now and again I feel that Ascendancy, feel that I become a part of it. But such moments are rare, extremely rare. And to make matters worse, those moments are so fleet and twinkling, I usually don't know they happened until later.

Those moments, I think, constitute what is commonly referred to as the creative experience.

Understand that I never look for that creative experience. I never try to be "creative." I never seek, nor wait for inspiration. I simply trundle along my old, familiar streets—working, digging through the garbage cans of any new and interesting mews I come upon. Tonight I will talk about one of my mews—the mew of the thief.

This time last year I was working on the illustrations for a book by Doris Orgel called *Ariadne, Awake!* I was dealing with all the problems which beset a project like that, namely the task of developing a cast of characters in which the heroes and heroines are attractive to the young reader and are represented in an historically accurate (or at least historically convincing) manner. And in like manner, the villains are represented as being appropriately unattractive.

In a book where I have to see a character several times, I usually hire a model to work with. For Ariadne, I used my assistant, Kate Kiesler. She was a wholesomely good-looking girl—red-headed, just about the right age, and she was available for the work. And besides, her mama researched and sewed up a real nice "Greek" gown for her to wear for the shoot.

For the minotaur I used my own corpulent body surmounted with a bloody bull's head. I also used my own figure for that of Daedalus working at his desk, drawing out the plans for the minotaur's labyrinth.

The rest of the characters I culled and pasted together from my collection of photographs of screen and stage actors and opera singers in costume. This is a common practice in my profession. We call such material "scrap." Using scrap is so common to this work that the library at Rhode Island School of Design has one full-time person and several work-study students to administer the school's clip file—a collection of scrap so large it occupies three rooms on the second floor of the library. There are also (I noticed in a recent catalog) clip files available on CD-ROM.

I teach at RISD. I teach there because I love to teach, actually—that and because it gets me off my hill and helps socialize me—and so I have access to that clip file. Those are three very good reasons to endure the four-hour commute back and forth to Providence every Wednesday.

The course I teach is called "Letters, Words, and Images." It is my attempt to expose a handful of senior illustration majors to the joys of letters and typography and to show them how letters and words relate to illustration in the creation of what is historically referred to as "the whole book." Here are a few of the early lessons I try to teach them. Lesson number one: There is no such thing as originality—especially with letters. I reinforce this intellectual and artistic conceit with two literary *bons-mots*—the first from Hart Crane when he said, "God damn this constant nostalgia always for something new." The second is a paraphrase of E. H. Gombrich: Art does not come from nature. Art comes from art.

Lesson number two: Illustration is a whore's profession. No matter how much we enjoy doing it we wouldn't do it unless we got paid money for it. We do it for "fun and profit," as Donald Hall puts it—and that's alright. It's honest.

And like unto that I teach them that illustration is a thief's profession. It is a thief's profession because we steal. We steal from the dead, we steal from the living, and we steal from ourselves.

And I adjure my young students, "When you're being a whore, you be a good one, an expensive one too, if you can muster it—and always make your 'John' think you enjoyed it as much as he did. And when you're being a thief, you be a good thief—don't get caught."

I got caught recently. Early last month I got a letter from Doris Orgel—actually it was a letter to her which she had photocopied for me and to which she had appended a few questions. The letter to her was from one Father Owen Lee.

Father Lee thanked Ms. Orgel for sending him a copy of *Ariadne*. He said that it was a special pleasure to find it waiting for him when he returned home from a trip. He complimented her on her suspenseful retelling of the tale, and for showing that, in his words, "there are always new ways of feeling one's way into myth."

Then he said that he was surprised by my portrait of King Minos, which he correctly identified as Wagner's first Tristan, Ludwig Schnorr von Carolsfeld—"from the hair and beard to the physique to the smallest details of the costume!"

Then Doris asked me if I were an opera lover and if what Father Lee said were true. She explained that Father Owen Lee is the erudite commentator on the Saturday afternoon Metropolitan Opera broadcasts and teaches classics at St. Michael's in Toronto. She said that she was very curious and asked me to please solve the mystery.

And thus I got caught pilfering from the Met archives! What cheek! How unoriginal! How uncreative! What a reprehensible scalawag I am!

So much for that.

Here's another story: two or three years ago a woman wrote to me saying that she had a friend who had long admired my work, but who had recently found cause to be disappointed—he found that I had used a Käthe Kollwitz self-portrait for one of my images of Biddy Early in Nancy Willard's *The Ballad of Biddy Early*. I imagine that she and her friend were expecting an apology or embarrassed explanation of some sort, but instead they got a short exegesis on creative thievery. For Biddy Early I needed the face of a woman at various stages in her life. Where do I find that? Well, I admire Kollwitz' work and know her self-portraits moderately well. She made them all through her life (from 1891 to 1942), so I commandeered three or four of them to use as my reference and model for Biddy's aging face. That one of the early self-portraits (1898) bears a resemblance to a beautiful woman of Irish extraction whom I fell in love with a long time ago is not unimportant—that resemblance made me feel comfortable in transposing a German Käthe Kollwitz into an Irish Biddy Early.

After explaining this I posed my own query: why, I asked, if the gentleman who impugned me were such a champion of the Kollwitz self-portraits, had he questioned only the very famous self-portrait I used? Was he not familiar with the lesser-known ones I quoted? I never got an answer.

I would note here that Kollwitz herself was not above a bit of pilfering. All one need do is compare the male nude in her etching *The Downtrodden* with Hans Holbein the Younger's 1521 painting of the *Dead Christ in the Tomb* which hangs in the Basle Museum. If she did not copy the figure directly, she surely saw it at some point in her life and was so struck by it she used it unconsciously—something all artists do. The first appearance of the Holbein figure I can find in her work is in an 1896 etching called *Reclining Male Nude*. She uses the same figure again that same year in an etching called *O People You Bleed from Many Wounds*. Then she quotes *O People You Bleed* in her 1900 etching and aquatint *The Downtrodden* (plates 5 & 6).

In her essay "Wearing the Other Hat," Mem Fox, the gifted Australian writer, catalogs her own bag of stolen goods. She used the rhyme scheme and the setting (grabbed unconsciously, she says) from "The Rime of the Ancient Mariner" for her book *Sail Away*. The last line of "Possum Magic," ('And she did') was "nicked quietly" from the story of *The Little Red Hen*. She also admits to "whipping" a couple of phrases straight from the Bible like "And it came to pass," and "In peace and unafraid." That Ms. Fox is incorrect about "in peace and unafraid" coming from the Bible—it does not, according to *Strong's Exhaustive Concordance*—underscores the fact that thieves like us often steal from sources we merely remember, and sometimes remember incorrectly.

All this stealing reminds me of the guy Alexander Pope wrote about in this little couplet:

Next o'r all his books his eyes began to roll
In pleasing memory of all he stole.

If calling myself (and my colleagues) a thief seems a bit harsh, then try the French word *bricoleur*. It is a term used to describe someone who works with discarded things—garbage, rubbish, flotsam, and jetsam. For me this means cast-off issues of *National Geographic*, family photographs in albums I buy at flea markets, old high school yearbooks, clippings from the local newspapers, and other similar materials.

I also use things that are estimable—photographs, paintings, drawings, and designs done by masters of the medium. I work variations on their themes. I borrow, steal, and quote self-portraits from Kollwitz, portraits of politicians and generals from Matthew Brady, a farm-woman from Dorothea Lange, a page of type from T. J. Cobden-Sanderson.

This is a practice which I think bears comparison to Beethoven's quotations of Handel in *Judas Maccabaeus*; Benjamin Britten's quotation of John Dowland's *O, Come Heavy Sleep* in Britten's *Opus 7 Nocturnal*; Mendelssohn's quotation of Bach's *A Mighty Fortress is our God* which Bach had taken from Martin Luther; Charles Ives' quotation of *America* in his *Variations on America*—a theme that, I am sure, was itself filched from somewhere or somebody. I recently heard a composition of Philip Glass in which, if I did not misunderstand the radio announcer, he had taken a theme from David Bowie.

And, if I may be so bold, it is no different from Jasper Johns' quoting my image of the great whale from *Moby-Dick* (plate 7) in his 1983 painting called *Ventriloquist*. As I was preparing this speech, I wrote to him and asked him what the title of the work was; I had forgotten. He wrote back, saying that indeed his painting included a partial tracing of my print, as do several other related works, two lithographs among them. He also noted that this has been mentioned frequently in print.

To go further, I would ask you to consider that not only do artists steal from other artists, they steal from themselves—like Kollwitz did. Similarly, Christopher Hogwood said about George Frederic Handel, that "Borrowing was a standard component of Handel's compositional technique. In *Messiah* he reused a number of his own secular compositions, especially a recently written set of Italian secular vocal duets. From this source comes most of the music of 'And He shall purify,' 'His Yoke is easy,' 'All we, like sheep,' and other vocal numbers." Great long chords of his *Hallelujah Chorus* can also be found in the oratorio *Joseph and His Brethren*. It appears, therefore, that many of the twenty-three days Handel spent writing that great, massive, and inspired work of his were spent rearranging and reconfiguring a lot of his old work previously published and performed.

An example of this from my own work is the illustration of "Undertaker" from a word histories book I illustrated called *From Quiche to Humble Pie*. The undertaker in *From Quiche to Humble Pie* is a variation on my image of the undertaker (plate 8) in my 1985 edition of *Adventures of Huckleberry Finn*, which is itself a variation on a photograph of the 19th century orator and statesman Henry Clay that was made by Matthew Brady.

Here's another example of my self-pilfering: Giant Despair (plate 20), from my *Pilgrim's Progress*: the image is a liquored-up giant slumped over a table with the remains of a human repast strewn on the floor around him. Originally the image was done as a wood-engraving to illustrate "Jack and the Beanstalk" for a 1985 Time-Life volume about giants and ogres. I recycled the image nearly ten years later making Jack's giant into John Bunyan's giant named Despair. The point of view is the same, the pose of the figure is the same, the costume is the same. But it is an entirely new image because I reversed everything so that what was on the left is now on the right—which was in fact the way I drew the image on the wood block to begin with. Then, I rendered the image in watercolor, which changed its aspect dramatically. And, then, I altered some of the details of the scene to accommodate the specifics of the new textual setting, namely some blood and bones of a recent repast. The result was an entirely new image—a variation on a theme—like Ives' *Variations on America*.

Now, someone in this room is wondering if, by doing this, I perhaps meant to suggest that the reader should ask the question "Is the blood-smelling giant of Jack's beanstalk the exact same giant, old Despair, that eats the flesh and gnaws the bones of Christian pilgrims?" The answer to the question: no, but it's an interesting thought and I wish I had come up with it. All it really means is that I recycled and re-rendered a giant.

Stealing can be carried to an extreme as things in our century and in our country often are. For instance, in New York a few years ago there was an avant-garde school of painters who called themselves, or who were called, "appropriationists." For all I know, they may still be at work. I don't keep up with the "movements" in the New York art scene, so I don't know. From what I have been told, their raison d'être was to copy (as perfectly as they could, I suppose) someone else's work and sign their own name to it—thereby "appropriating" the image as their own. I am sure they sold well to very keen art collectors who keep up with the scene. I do not imagine, however, that many appropriated Vermeer, Velásquez, or Veronese.

Nevertheless, artistic appropriation and reconfiguration has been the ways and means of "creative" people for a very long time. In fact, Terence, writing in Rome in the second century BCE, told us not only that charity begins at home and that we should exercise moderation in all things, but (in the Prologue to *The Eunuch*) he told us that "nothing is said that has not been said before." A more recent example is a story someone told me about a snotty critic asking Johannes Brahms if he didn't think his symphonies were very much like Beethoven's. Brahms retorted stoutly, "Yes, any fool could tell that." The same attitude, with a bit of a twist on it, is evident in Tchaikovsky's reply when he too was accused of purloining from Beethoven. His response was as terse as Brahms'. He said, "I have a right. I love him."

When I was talking with my friend Paul Mariani about these matters, he reminded me that some birds do the same thing—they take over a live nest or commandeer an abandoned one and reconfigure it into something entirely new, something they can use. Civilizations too, Mariani noted, pick preceding civilizations to the bones, digesting and reconfiguring what they find useful into their own forms, forms that fit their own needs.

Three years ago Harcourt Brace commissioned me to do eight paintings for the covers of their newly-designed series of the fiction of Eudora Welty. They also asked me to write a short piece about the paintings for their catalog. This is what I wrote:

"Had Mark Twain made tintypes of life on the Mississippi around 1875, any latter-day illustrator of, say, the *Adventures of Huckleberry Finn* would be remiss, if not indeed downright neglectful, not to seek them out, absorb them, and let them freely influence the subject, mood, timbre, density, and color of his pictures. Eudora Welty has given us just such a photographic legacy, and I have tapped into it unabashedly (believing as I do that originality is a result, not a task). In doing the paintings for the front covers of the newly designed Harvest editions of her fiction, I isolated certain figures in her photographs from their periphery; I recomposed them; I married elements of one picture to elements of another or to elements of pictures by other limners of that time and place: Ben Shahn, Marion Post Wolcott, Doris Ullman, Walker Evans. Quoting and paraphrasing as I have done, it seems to me, not only makes the illustrations authentic but also fulfills a responsibility to Miss Welty's vision and pays homage to the extraordinary photographic work of one of America's great artists."

When I asked Miss Welty if she objected to my using her photographs as I did, she said, as she clapped her hands together, "Oh, no, Barry, I think it's just wonderful what you've done with them."

In his essay, "The Paradoxes of Creativity," Jacques Barzun says that creativity, to most people, is an idea that means "producing something where nothing was before—making a thing out of nothing. But the same people who take that meaning for granted also believe from common sense and the teachings of science that nothing can be made from nothing: every object or creature is only the transformation of some preexisting thing." Later in his essay he points out that "no word is put to more frequent and varied use than 'creativity.'"

In a fit of "creativity" I took Barzun's lead and did a search for "The Creative" in my favorite source of all—the telephone book. Here are the results of my fit.

In Amherst, Massachusetts, I found, there is Creative Carpentry and The Creative Needle.

In Hadley, Massachusetts there are Creative Tee Shirts.

In Easthampton, Massachusetts there are Creative Display Fixtures.

In Chattanooga, Tennessee you have Creative Cakes Catering & Flowers, Creative Day Care for the Elderly, Creative Engineering, Creative Fabric, Creative Iron, Creative Management, Creative Metals, and Creative Photography by T. Fred.

In Jackson, Mississippi one can find a Creative Learning Center, Creative Packaging, a Creative Shop (now there's a head-scratcher), a Creative Spirit Studio, Creative Systems Consultants, and a Creative Tool & Millworks.

I have to add that all these Jacksonian creators are followed in the book by Crechale's—a roadhouse out on Highway 80 that is, or used to be, truly creative in their preparation of fried chicken gizzards.

Unless I read the books incorrectly, there is nothing creative in either Sherman, Texas or in Fulton, Mississippi.

I picked up the New Orleans phone book to see what I could find, but I put it right back down because I have done carried this thing far enough. As Barzun says, "The magic of the word 'creative' is so broad that no distinct meaning need be attached to it; it fits all situations, pointing to nothing in particular." Indeed, I think that "being creative" falls pretty much in the same league with being "talented." Both wonderments are as common as house dust and just about as valuable.

It is a fact that no one ever made a wood engraving or wrote a sestina by merely being creative. That's like a tail wagging a dog, for God's sake. Rather than teaching kids to be "creative" they should be taught what art really is. They should be taught the history of its practitioners, and a good deal about the role craftsmanship plays in the process. They should be taught form, not finger paints. They should be taught that art, contrary to the conventional wisdom, is not self-indulgent. They should be taught that art does not come to those who wait. They should be taught that art comes from those who do—that the very genius of art lies in action. In doing.

They should be taught that art comes from study and from hard work and from solid craftsmanship; they should know that beyond determination and persistence, art comes about only through study, work, and knowledge of their craft.

I taught high school for twenty-five years. I have no record of how many students I taught over all those years, but it has to be in the tens of hundreds. Based on that experience I can say honestly that I never met a student who was not "creative," nor did I ever meet one who was not "talented." A few of those students are now professional graphic designers, painters, architects, potters, and furniture makers. But why them and not the others, if, as I say, all of them were creative and talented?

The answer is simple: some of my students persisted and some did not. Those who did not persist were the ones lacking sufficient interest, drive, and discipline. Those who did persist persisted because they had energy, they had courage (or "sand" as my grandaddy would have put it), and they developed a need to work.

Moser's three rules for the so-called creative life are, therefore,

Persistence.

Indefatigable energy.

The habit of work.

Far too many kids are herded unnecessarily into an intellectual abattoir—spurred along by well-meaning but shortsighted and under-informed parents, teachers, aunts, uncles, brothers, and sisters who remind the kid that cows aren't purple (as if the kid had made a purple cow rather than a picture of a purple cow). Those who persist in the face of these barriers are the ones who have the courage. Without courage the imaginative and inventive kid does not survive to become an imaginative and inventive adult.

I was told in grammar school that I should never draw with a ruler, because, as Mrs. Colett said, "Artists don't use rulers." So I didn't use a ruler.

I was told by an otherwise encouraging Mrs. Turner that I shouldn't trace pictures because, as she said, "Real artists don't trace pictures, sugar."

I wonder how that lovely woman thinks Jasper Johns could have gotten that big whale from *Moby-Dick* onto his seven foot high *Ventriloquist*? As noted earlier, he traced it.

I spent six years at the military school from which I graduated in 1958. Creative skills held a low priority. No art classes were taught. No "creative" writing classes either, not that I remember. There was a mechanical drawing course (good for all those aspiring engineers), and we diagrammed a lot of sentences—skills I must say in all fairness, that I find useful to this very day. I suppose the attitude in military school was that "creative" thinking would be anathema to the military conformity they instilled in us: line up, follow orders, and don't question authority. And besides, as we all knew back then, art was not a manly thing to teach to all those young southern lords. Sure, it was okay for the little ladies over at Girls' Preparatory School, but not for us Baylor boys.

During those same years, I was indoctrinated by a family—a loving family—who told me plainly that I shouldn't try to become an artist because I would never be able to "make a living at it." After all, my daddy's boss's son had tried and he couldn't do it—he ended up selling life insurance—and, my family reasoned, I wouldn't be able to do any better. My family was wrong. They failed to factor into their equation pluck, energy, determination, and work habits.

In college I was told to never use photographs in my paintings that I had not made myself. Leonard Baskin still criticizes me from time to time for being too dependent on photographs. I take his criticism with a smile and a grain of salt—his illustration of *The Owl That Calls Upon the Night* from the Gehenna Press edition of William Blake's *Auguries of Innocence* was taken rather directly from a photograph of a spectacled owl found on page eighty-four of *Birds of Other Lands* published in 1917 by the University Society. Parenthetically, it is interesting to note that same owl was in turn pilfered by Brad Holland for an illustration which appeared in *Playboy* magazine in the early 70's—Holland made Baskin's owl a Holland owl by giving it a peg leg with a buxom nude hugging up to it. Otherwise it was a fairly accurate copy. But perhaps in the long run, Leonard is right about my being too dependent on photographs. I don't know. I don't care. They get me where I want to go.

And you know what? I trace too—I have a little room in my studio that was built for the sole purpose of tracing.

And you know what else? I use a lot of rulers and t-squares and triangles too, because sometimes only straight lines and square corners will do.

In short, I will do whatever I need to do or have to do—and use whatever I have to use—to get the work done to my specifications and expectations. Nobody else's. That's the ultimate reward of this life, no longer having to work toward, or according to, anyone else's particulars. It's emancipation, and it's hard won. And it's a reparation of sorts, a wondrous recompense for persistence, pluck, and a willingness to fail.

Fairy Tales & Good Bourbon Whiskey

The First Eudora Welty Film & Fiction Festival
Jackson, Mississippi
May 3, 1996

I MET EUDORA WELTY in Jackson, Mississippi on May 21, 1986. Our mutual friends, John and Mel Evans, drove me to her house to make the introduction. John had been determined for some time that Miss Welty and I should collaborate on a book, so he approached her asking if she would be interested in such an undertaking. As John told me later, she was very happy with the idea, and he took it upon himself to arrange a meeting the next time I was in Jackson.

So here we were, walking up the front walk, across her tree-shaded and well-kept lawn. The front door of the vestibule opened, and a small voice said, "Hey, Johnny. Hey, Mel." Then, as she held open the screen door for us, Johnny said, "Miss Eudora, I'd like for you to meet Barry Moser." She offered me her hand, and said, "Oh, Barry, I am so pleased to meet you." I took her small hand in mine, saying that I was very pleased to meet her too. And then I handed her a gift, a bottle of the finest bourbon whiskey I knew at that time: W. L. Weller 107 proof, also known as "Old Weller." We were still standing outside when I said, "Miss Welty, I know that this is a bit odd for one southerner to bring another southerner a bottle of southern whiskey bought way up yonder in New England, but I understand that you like Bourbon whiskey." She smiled, eyes twinkling, and rubbed her hands together. "Oh, indeed I do," she said.

So having broken the ice—and subsequently breaking open that bottle of Weller—we all went inside. She showed us to the front parlor where the cool, tree-dappled light came in through the windows. Books were everywhere in neat stacks, on the floor, on the tables. Before she sat down to visit, she asked us if she could get us something to eat. Of course, we said no—we didn't want her going to any trouble. So she went to the kitchen and brought out some glasses and ice. We opened that bottle of Weller and sat and sipped whiskey and chatted about this and that, during which time Miss Welty asked—more than a few times—if she could get us something to eat. Finally, she addressed the issue we had all come to talk about. She asked, "So tell me, Barry, what book of mine are you the most interested in illustrating?" The answer came without hesitation, "*The Robber Bridegroom*," I said. I explained to her that it had long been a favorite of mine, and I knew it would lend itself to my style of illustration. She clapped her hands and said, "Oh, I was hoping you'd say that!" So we talked about it for a while and then the conversation moved on to other things, as conversations do. And when it was time to leave and we were all saying our good-byes at the front door, Miss Welty said, "Well, it certainly was a nice visit this afternoon, but I sure do wish you all had eaten some of those sandwiches I fixed."

The next year, we published our collaboration at Pennyroyal Press: the illustrations printed from the original engraving blocks (plate 9), bound in full leather, and printed letterpress in an edition of 150 copies. Harcourt Brace Jovanovich published a trade edition in 1991.

As I was worked on *The Robber Bridegroom*, three things struck me about Miss Welty's retelling of the Grimm tale: first, she set it in Mississippi; second, she told it about real people; and third, she used language that seemed to come from the people themselves and not from any literary precept or convention. Interestingly enough, these were the very things the Grimm brothers themselves were celebrated for championing and engendering in their work. A few years later these same three issues came to roost in the hen house of my own imagination when I was asked to write my first retelling of a fairy tale.

When that happened I was not exactly new to writing. I had been writing incidental, "scholarly" stuff in the form of speeches, essays, and long notes about my work as an illustrator on such projects as *The Divine Comedy*, *Moby-Dick*, *Alice's Adventures in Wonderland*, and the like. But I had never attempted fiction. I had no aspirations or ambitions in that direction at all. I had always imagined that if my career were ever to take a different tack it would be toward sculpture. But life, as we know all too well, sometimes goes in unexpected directions, and in 1989 Maria Modugno, my editor at Little, Brown and Company, commissioned me to do an illustrated retelling of Hans Christian Andersen's *The Tinderbox*.

Now, to be sure, I am not afraid of doing something new. In fact, every time I begin a project I feel like I am starting from scratch, that I don't really know what I'm doing. But this was a particularly scary challenge. I hadn't done this kind of storytelling before, so I accepted the challenge with an important caveat—that if what I wrote wasn't any good, Maria would pull me out of it and write it herself or get somebody else to do it.

I struggled with it for a long time and wrote nothing that was worth remembering or keeping out of the trash can. When I despaired, Maria spurred me on. She told me to stop writing and tell the story to my children in my own words. She told me to record it and transcribe the spoken words. I did exactly as she said. I told it to my kids and to Jane Dyer's kids, Brooke and Cecily, who were closer to the age of the intended audience than my daughters or my granddaughters were. But every time I told it, it not only sounded disingenuous to me, it bored the beejeesus out of the kids. It sounded awful. Every time I spoke or wrote about a copper castle or a dog with eyes the size of saucers or a king or a princess I stumbled. I don't know any castles. Nor princesses. Nor kings. But I do know mountains—the

Cumberlands, the Blue Ridge, the Berkshires. And I know American heroes and heroines—Thomas Jefferson, Helen Keller, Martin Luther King. And American myths, too—the stories of John Henry, Paul Bunyan, Rip Van Winkle. So I began wondering if I shouldn't use an American idiom, as Miss Welty did in *The Robber Bridegroom*, to frame my adaptation of this story. And as I was meditating on this it began to bother me that in all the children's books I knew, tales of magic and mystery seemed to happen only in times long gone and in places very far away.

Then, as all this new cogitation was settling into my bones, a very strange thing happened: I heard the story inside my head. I heard it as if my Aunt Velma, long since dead, were telling me the story. Telling it to me as if I were sitting on that old green glider on that screened-in front porch watching her cigarette glow and dance in the dark as she talked. This was language I was comfortable with. It was the language that years of education had sought to cleanse and rid me of—malapropisms, double negatives and "might could's." This is when I learned that language is a manifestation of place.

So I started my retelling of *The Tinderbox* fresh from the point of view of language—the language of my people.

Through it all I stayed true to the essence of Andersen's telling. My version, like Andersen's, is a tale of wonder and magic. It is a story of a soldier going home after a war, finding wealth, losing it, finding it again, and along the way discovering a great truth: that important things, like faith and trust, love and friendship, are beyond wealth.

That I set the story in America—specifically the Cumberland Plateau—fell quite naturally into place after my linguistic epiphany. It also followed quite naturally that I set it in the not-so-distant past—the nineteenth century at the end of the Civil War. Not that I am an authority on the "recent unpleasantness." In fact, I am not particularly interested in it. I took the War for granted because my childhood was spent on the slow eastern slope of Missionary Ridge, one of the bloodiest battlegrounds of the war. Caissons, cannons and stone soldiers were among my playthings.

But that's where I saw my hero, making his way up the valley between Lookout Mountain and Missionary Ridge. Saw him as I see all my memories. He was a Confederate soldier who came from somewhere like Sequatchie, Tennessee, or maybe over in Jasper, or maybe Soddy-Daisy. And then I saw my heroine, not as a princess at all, but a green-eyed country girl, likely of Scotch or Irish extraction, who wore a dress that came from somewhere up the river in Ohio or maybe Illinois.

The witch was a problem. Not that she was difficult to envision, on the contrary. It's just that I have three daughters and four grand daughters and am sensitive to the roles of women in my books. There is far too much violence done to women in our society today without my fostering or perpetuating it in my work. So, since the demise of the witch is central to the story and I couldn't simply dispense with her, I gave her a sex-change and made her into an ogre. An old curmudgeon. An East Tennessee mountain man, like the one who took a shot at me and my friends when we accidentally got too close to his still.

The Tinderbox was published in 1990. One reviewer (writing in the *School Library Journal*) said that purists would be horrified, because this was not just a retelling but a complete re-imagining of the tale. Indeed, *The Horn Book* said that it was "inaccurate to credit Andersen as the author." What happened was that the story took a new form in my Aunt Velma's East Tennessee twang. I had done nothing more than what Andersen himself had done. What the Grimms had done. What Miss Welty had done. I did not merely change the clothes of an old story, but I changed its voice and its place.

After *The Tinderbox* came a retelling of the old British ballad, *Polly Vaughn* (1992) That, in turn, was followed by retellings of *Rumpelstiltskin* (called *Tucker Pfeffercorn*, 1994), and *The Gift of the Magi* (called *Good and Perfect Gifts*, 1997). All three stories were commissioned by Maria Modugno, who, after having pushed me into this terra incognita, continued to provide me with the new and necessary tools to explore it. And like *The Tinderbox*, these later stories were set in East Tennessee, and all the characters spoke a lot like my Aunt Velma and my Uncle Floyd. Spoke with the voice of screen doors, good bourbon whiskey, and warm summer nights, not so far away, and not so long ago.

THE WHOLE BOOK

A speech given at the American Bookseller's Convention
Anaheim, California
May 23, 1992

ON THE 8TH OF MAY, 1932, George Bernard Shaw wrote a brief but telling letter to a young illustrator named John Farleigh. Shaw wrote at the suggestion of his publisher, William Maxwell, who knew Farleigh's work and thought that the addition of his wood engravings to Shaw's story, *The Black Girl in Her Search for God*, would make the book both more attractive and more marketable. So Mr. Shaw wrote to Farleigh saying:

Dear Sir
As I am old and out of date, I have not the privilege of knowing you or your work. But Mr. William Maxwell of Clark's of Edinburgh tells me that you can design, draw and engrave pictures as parts of a printed book, which, you will understand, is something more than making a picture and sticking it into a book as an "illus-

tration." The idea is that you and I and Maxwell should co-operate in turning out a good looking little volume consisting of the story contained in the enclosed proof sheets ... and say, a dozen pictures.

Are you sufficiently young and unknown to read the story and make one trial drawing for me for five guineas? That is if the job interests you?

> *Faithfully,*
> *G. Bernard Shaw*

Looking at this letter closely, I find several things of interest.

First, Shaw not only realized that Farleigh would immediately understand that illustrating a book was "something more than making a picture and sticking it in," but he also recognized that designing, drawing, and engraving were all inseparable parts of a printed book. In this letter, Shaw implied an important concept, a philosophy, if you will, which is the very core of my work: The Whole Book.

By "the whole book" I mean this: Books are made of paper, type, ink, bindings, and a text—which sometimes, though not always, benefits from illustrations. "The whole book" is one wherein the materials, text, design, and pictures are so coherently joined that not one of the parts can be separated from it without diminishing the whole or even the parts themselves. For me, a book is what a painting is for a painter—a thoughtfully conceived and carefully executed object; an adroit arrangement of plastic elements; a coherent and intelligent marriage of text, type, and image.

The second thing of interest in Shaw's letter comes when he notes to Farleigh that "The idea is that you and I and Maxwell should co-operate in turning out *a good looking little volume* [italics mine]." Now, outside of writing stories and novels, bookmaking, like architecture and filmmaking, is inherently social in nature. It is unlike the solitary nature of say, painting and sculpture, which requires nothing of anyone else but the artist (except, of course, suppliers of utilities and manufacturers of paraphernalia, and even these are not always a given). In bookmaking there must be collegiality and a co-operation, as Shaw put it, between author, editor, and illustrator. Indeed, bookmaking mandates co-operation not only between author, publisher, editor, and illustrator, but also with art director, typographer, marketing director, production manager, paper supplier, printer, binder, distributor, and eventually the bookseller.

This is not to say, however, that I, or others like me, do not while away countless hours alone. We do. Our craft demands it. But the daily solitude is punctuated by frequent phone calls from editors, art directors, colleagues, friends, and production managers creating new projects, reconciling editorial issues, swapping recipes, correcting chromalins, adjusting typography, choosing binding materials, commiserating about deadlines or parenthood, or writing flap copy. No book can be produced without this kind of constant and flexible co-operation.

The third thing in Shaw's letter I want to highlight is something that my Mamma always told me was impolite to talk about in public: money. Shaw brings up this ugly matter when he queries Farleigh, "Are you sufficiently young and unknown to … make one trial drawing for me for five guineas?"

Now, I am not going to say that I work simply to make money. Mind you, it is precisely the sort of thing I could say just to be ornery or iconoclastic. In fact, I could polish my ornery iconoclasm with historic bons-mots. For instance, did you know that Raphael based his fresco fees on a per-head basis? That Rubens invented the painting production line to earn greater sums of remuneration (and subsequently became astonishingly wealthy)? Or that Titian lived in his own palace? Of course, we don't even want to begin talking about composers and writers! But if I were to say that about myself, it would be disingenuous. While I certainly work for money, much like the artists I just mentioned, there is a higher purpose that calls me to my craft. But—that "higher purpose" is not the ennobling of the human spirit, nor the enrichment of man's existence, nor any such self-serving, self-aggrandizing hogwash. It is, quite simply, in sculptor David Smith's words, an arrogant need to create.

And this overriding need to create has afforded me some unusual critical receptions. For example, on January 21, 1991, writing in the Book World column of the *Washington Post*, David Streitfeld said: "Barry Moser is so prolific he could form his own book of the month club." In the next sentence he feels he has to drive his point further home: "Moser has his detractors who say that he works too fast...."

Now, I'm not given to taking critics too seriously. I am much of the same mind as Max Reger when he responded to a critic by writing the following, "Sir, I am sitting in the smallest room in my house, I have your review in front of me. Soon it will be behind me." Nevertheless, Mr. Streitfeld's comments do give me an interesting—if unintended—platform from which to make a few observations.

It is true that I have been involved one way or another in the production of a number of books—over two hundred so far—but it seems that taking note of my productivity is the limit of my critic's observation. Had he considered the nature of my productivity more carefully, he may have come up with other more interesting things to say. For instance:

"Mr. Moser must love little children to do so many books for them."

Had he written this, I would respond, yes, I do love children, but I do not make books for them any more than I make books for adults. Ten years ago, if anyone told me that I would be speaking at the 1992 ABA as a writer and illustrator of children's books, I would have found it amusing and would have thought it hardly likely. My life at the time was immersed in making *livres d'artiste*, illustrating *Moby-Dick*, *The Divine Comedy*, *The Æneid*, *The Odyssey*, and illustrating the poetry of David Smith, William Stafford, and Paul Mariani. I was also up to my adenoids producing a folio *Alice in Wonderland* at my own Pennyroyal Press. But even my *Alice* with its nightmare-like illustrations, scholarly shoulder notes, and a final portrait of Alice naked, was not envisioned as a book for children. It was, as are all my books, created with me as the audience. For I believe with such artists as Goethe, Flannery O'Connor, and Alfred Kazin that first, I work to entertain myself; second, I write and draw in order to find out what I'm thinking; and third, in all I do, I seek to understand. To satisfy some deep and curious part of my soul. If someone else enjoys my work, or is transported to another time and place, or is amused by it, or perhaps even benefits from it, well, that's a dividend. Because for me it is all a matter of satisfying that arrogant need to create.

Consider also that my critic could have said, in conjunction with my "detractors" who say that I work too fast, "I wonder what would happen if Moser worked slower?"

And I would respond, "Hell, budrow, I can't work any slower."

My workday is pretty much like everybody else's—up in the morning, work all day, relax at night, and then go to bed. I don't begin my workday at 4 a.m. like I used to, and I don't work nights any more, keeping my evenings, as Eudora Welty says, for family and friends. And yet, I'm more productive now than I was when I worked those insane, grueling hours—perhaps that says something about experience, maturity, and the unacknowledged benefits of grey hair.

But anyhow—what exactly is it about making so many books that bothers people? Had I stayed a painter (which is what I was trained for) and had I spent all my hours developing a comparable visual fluency and versatility whereby critics would review my paintings as they do my books, I daresay no critic would ever accuse me of being overly prolific if I produced only six or eight paintings a year! Apparently book critics see productivity in a different light. And it is a serious "misreading" of the book maker's work, for making books is no more nor less a complex and profound an activity than making paintings.

Then, consider this: the critic could have said, "Moser must love his work to do so much of it." And I would respond, "Yes, I do love my work." As Matisse said, work is paradise. My love for my work and my love for my children are the twin engines that drive my life. There is never a morning that I do not look forward to hugging and kissing my kids, and (after the coffee is made and the dogs are fed), getting down to work. I look forward to my work because, for one thing, my work comes easily to me, as I am sure composing music came easily to Georg Philipp Telemann. And in this, I join the ranks of most of the artists I know.

In fact, I did a private poll of some artist and writer friends a few years ago. I asked them this simple question: "Is it easy for you to write (or illustrate) books? At first, Jane Yolen, Cynthia Rylant, Jane Dyer, and Patty MacLachlan, among others, all resisted my request that they answer with a simple yes or no, but when I pushed and nagged them—and confessed to them that it was easy for me—they all answered in kind. Yes, they all agreed, it was easy for them. And if you stop to think about it, it has to be. How else could Telemann have written over forty operas, 600 overtures, and over sixty settings of the Passion of Christ? It's what he did every day. It's what all artists and writers do. We make things. And if the very act of making things were a constant difficulty every time we started exploring a new idea then we would never get beyond our medium and into the idea. I think that's what William Faulkner alluded to when he said that all he needed to do his work was "paper, tobacco, food, and a little whiskey." But let me say, as my friends said to me in resisting my question, that while it's easy for writers to write, and for painters to paint, it is not easy for writers or painters to write or paint well. No matter how good the writer or painter may be, writing and painting *well* is a gut-wrenching experience. Not only do we have to make our materials behave the way we want them to (which is not always the way *they* want to), we also have to enter into a cheerless and contentious battle with the most devastating critic there is—the "inner critic" as Ben Shahn calls it—the one that lives inside your viscera, inside your brain and heart.

At the Rhode Island School of Design, where I sometimes teach, I criticize my students' work with generosity, kindness, and a sensitivity to their needs. But when I criticize my own work, I am abject, insensitive, ruthless, and—sometimes—destructive. I know of no critic who would rip or shred or burn one of my paintings or engravings, regardless of how much he hated it. Yet ripping, wadding, shredding, and burning are commonplace, almost ritual, events in my studio. If my *Washington Post* critic knew how much work I destroyed in the course of a day, he would probably faint away in a paroxysm of astonishment.

Finally, consider this: my critic could have said, "Moser must have a big mortgage to have to make so many books." Now had he said this, I would have thought him well above average in perception. I do have a big mortgage, and I have that big mortgage precisely because, as our critic has it, I am prolific—or, as I see it, because I work hard. Remember that George Bernard Shaw asked John Farleigh not if he were willing to make a trial drawing for him, but if he would be willing to make a trial drawing for him *for five guineas*. Shaw understood better than most that art is damned hard work and not a charitable enterprise.

And remember, too, that Shaw and Maxwell employed Farleigh's talents not for the sake of art nor because Shaw so admired Farleigh's work, but to the make the book more marketable.

Quibbles with critics aside, let me conclude by saying that making illustrated books, as Mr. Shaw quite rightly observed, is a great deal more than making pictures and sticking them into a book as "illustrations." The whole book is a richly complex undertaking, one in which co-operation between the sundry parties involved is paramount, and one in which knowledge of history, and art, and technology are indispensable. But it is not, as Shaw also observed, a philanthropy. I need to make enough money each month so that I can continue to make more books. My publishers need to turn a profit so they can stay in business and produce more books. And you, the booksellers, need to sell enough books to pay your staffs and maintain your stores so you can sell more books. And though it may go without saying, I believe that most of us—authors, illustrators, publishers, booksellers—are in this business because we love books and are dedicated to them. And not just to books either, but to good books. And good books, as George Moore said, are invincible things, neither malice nor stupidity can crush them.

ON COLLABORATION

ILLUSTRATION, AS UNDERSTOOD in terms of the whole book, is more akin to filmmaking, theater, and architecture than it is to painting, sculpture, or poetry in that it is a collegial and social art; it is collaboration and conspiracy. In the broadest sense illustration involves editors, publishers, paper-makers, printers, binders, distributors, booksellers, and consumers. Even in the narrowest sense it involves others like paper-makers, or in the case of engraved illustration, the block maker. Even though most of my working day is spent alone, working for all intents and purposes as a solitary painter or printmaker, my mind is focused on the whole book and I am never far away from the telephone, e-mail, or the fax machine, nor outside the delivery and pick-up range range of Federal Express, UPS, or G.O.D. I cannot do a book alone. An illustration, yes. A book, no.

Two examples:

In 1978 I illustrated *Moby-Dick* (plate 7). The conditions of the commission were very specific: first, the images were to be accurate to the period when Melville put out to sea on the whaler *Acushnet*, which I believe was from 1841 to 1843 or thereabouts; secondly, they were to be documentary rather than narrative—something like providing stage sets, lights, costumes, and props. No actors. No performance. I was made well aware that it was to be a typographic book, not an illustrated book.

To these ends each engraved image was preceded by a detailed drawing which was photocopied and mailed to five authorities on Yankee whaling for validation and substantiation, as well as to the publisher who said yea or nay to the subject and composition of the images and who broke any stalemates among the authorities. Having the curators of whaling museums around the country perusing my work with the sole intent of finding mistakes, and an editor who had control over the content of the final compositions, was, to say the least, an uncomfortable prospect, so, needless to say, I did my homework, which included a lot of reading about ships and boats, whales and men, and the industrial techniques of Yankee whaling.

The idea was that the authorities would study the sketches, make their comments, and whatever quorum there was would hold sway. I had no reason to question their expertise—even though I had to do some images over and over to get them right—especially in such issues as the way line coils into a tub, how many men were in a whaleboat when it was lowered from the davits, the right kind of harpoons, and accurate depictions of rigging, rope-strapped blocks, and sails. But then there was the life-buoy.

Melville describes it as a "long, slender cask" with "studded iron bands" which hung at the stern "obedient" to "a cunning spring." He goes on, but even if Melville were trustworthy in his nautical descriptions, which he wasn't, there was nothing in this description to help me out much. I was under a lot of pressure to have a certain number of sketches in the committee's hands by a specific date and I was looking for something quick, small, and easy to fill out my quota. The only references I found to life-buoys were ones that were too late for the chronological framework, so I did what any good illustrator would do—I made it up. I reasoned that if it were thrown overboard it would be too smooth to hold onto, so I drew a couple of pieces of line riveted to the studded iron hoops. I imagined that such an attachment would give a drowning sailor something to grab hold of and it would be something that a ship's cooper and blacksmith could easily fabricate.

I had no clue as to what the cunning spring that the cask was obedient to might have been, but I reasoned that it must have been some kind of connector device. I couldn't figure out how to attach the life-line to the cask or the cunning spring, so I simply raised the cask up and looked at it from beneath, thereby skirting the problem entirely.

The drawing was sent out for inspection.

As I remember, three of the experts made no comment. One said "good," and one said that Moser had made the hoops on the cask too wide. Well, either Moser is a genius or else there is much to be questioned in academia. I assure you, Moser is not a genius.

But collaboration is not always so constricting. Indeed, it can be a joy.

Take for instance my collaboration with Nancy Willard on her retelling of Madame Leprince de Beaumont's *Beauty and the Beast*.

Our editor teamed us up and put us under contract before either of us had done a lick of work. Nancy, a friend of many years, called me and asked if I had any thoughts about the story. I told her, no, except that I would prefer seeing it set in America, perhaps at the turn of the century.

I felt strongly about this issue, and had already written about it in the afterword to my retelling of Hans Christian Andersen's *The Tinderbox*. As it happened, Nancy had already decided to set her *Beauty and the Beast* on the Hudson River and to use the great economic depression of 1893-94 as the framework for the father's loss of fortune. Our very first step was in independent concert with one another.

At Christmas that year, 1989, Nancy sent me an inscribed print of a photograph that her husband, Eric Lindbloom, had made of a splendid, run-down old Victorian mansion called Wilderstien, in Rhinebeck, New York. The inscription reads, "Dear Barry: A good house for the Beast, eh? We'll visit it in the spring. Happy New Year ... Nancy."

And indeed we did visit Wilderstien in the spring. It sits on a beautifully landscaped hill not far from Hyde Park overlooking the Hudson River. The crotched and gnarly Adirondacks loom on the horizon. Nancy and I met and walked in the gardens and through the house. We explored the stables and the carriage house, the attic and the towers. We opened one of the curved windows of the great cupola and walked out onto the rooftops. We told the story and parts of the story back and forth to each other. "Oh, look," Nancy said, "here's where they sit and play chess." And "Here is where Beauty stands and looks out at the distant hills, longing for home."

In one room we found an old heliogravure reproduction of one of Edward Hicks' *Peaceable Kingdom* paintings which became a motif in the story, as did the dragon-headed andirons we found in the parlor fireplace. We had tea in the parlor with Miss Daisy Suckley in whose family Wilderstien had been for generations. She raised Scottish Terriers and had given one to her neighbor, Franklin D. Roosevelt. She told us of the family and the history of the house. It was perfect and reminded me of Jean Cocteau's response to finding Roscherbon — "Everything is already there," he said, the "hidden rightness shines through the walls. All that we have to do is move the sun."

All day I took snapshots. Later, when they were developed, I copied them and sent them to Nancy along with photocopies of pictures I had culled from my collection of medical books—reconstructed faces, birth defects, cranio-facial deformities, burn victims, casualties of war—the sources I would be calling upon to invent my Beast. I did not want my Beast to be even vaguely attractive or handsome. Cocteau did that and did it better than I could. Walt Disney took the *beau idéal* to an absurdity. His Beast, I should think if I were a woman, might be interesting to lie with and have carnal knowledge of. He had good shoulders.

Not my Beast.

My Beast was originally conceived as a self-portrait because of a thing I do in black tie at Halloween. But that impulse eventually petered out because it was frivolous. Sometimes self-portraiture just doesn't work. But the Beast, *ma Bête*, remained human, entirely human, and therefore all the more repulsive (plate 10). He dressed well, a vestige of the *beau idéal* perhaps, but underneath the tuxedo he was, like Frankenstein's demon, ripe and repugnant.

Nancy took these images and sifted them with her notes of our conversations and exploration and tea with Miss Suckley and with her memories of that spring day above the Hudson River and wrote her version of the classic story.

Of our working together Nancy wrote:

"When I agreed to write a new version of *Beauty and the Beast* for Barry Moser to illustrate, I never dreamed that the story would open the door to a collaboration between us. Perhaps we would not have worked so closely on the book if we hadn't been introduced to …Wilderstien…. Indeed, the house was full of beasts, disguised as andirons, newel posts, and table legs. As Barry and I explored the house, not a single one escaped his notice.

"There is something of the fairy tale in [Moser's] transformation of what the real world gives him into detail that pulls you into the world of the story: an andiron, a staircase, a paw…"

In the Face of Presumptions

REGARDING ART IN EDUCATION

Art derives a considerable part of its beneficial exercise from flying in the face of presumptions. —Henry James, THE ART OF FICTION, *1888*

WE TEACH ART for the same reason we teach physics, Latin, calculus, or geography. Not a lot of people will agree with me, I'm sure, but that's to be expected because there is a persistent prejudice against art as an academic subject of equal "weight" as, say, Latin or calculus. Make no mistake about it, it is a matter of prejudice, and prejudice is a manifestation of ignorance, and Americans are, by and large, ignorant about art—witness, if you will, Senator Jesse Helms' nescient and parochial tirades about art on the Senate floor.

Why the debate goes on about the place of art in secondary education beats me, because teaching art, like teaching math, French, or trigonometry, exposes students to new ways of seeing, reasoning, and thinking. Art is not, contrary to public perception, a panacea for the learning-impaired. An art class is not a creative play period, or at least it shouldn't be. It is not a fuzzy, touchy-feely arena for kids who can't do anything else.

Art teaches us is that all objects, both natural and artificial, have in common certain things: notably, design, the relationship between form and function, and the fact that the act of creation is never completed. Art also teaches us, as Ben Shahn says in *The Shape of Content*, that there "is no content of knowledge which will not be important to the work [the young artist] will want to do." The more one learns about biology the more one understands the *ottava rima*. The more one reads Virgil, Homer, and Dante, the more one sees and understands the paintings of Bellini, Velásquez, and Kline. Art is not a frill, and any society that believes it is wades in a dangerous cultural cesspool.

The goal of teaching art in secondary education is not to make artists out of students any more than the goal of teaching biology and economics is to make doctors or politicians. The goal of education is, *per se*, to form integrated human beings. And we do this by exposing kids to as many of the probities of the human mind, the human heart, and the human experience as possible so that they are better equipped to make viable, exciting, and intelligent choices in directing the course of their lives. Individuals cannot be well educated and integrated with manipulated and limited data. Only by being exposed to all the disciplines can a student even hope to properly filter and process data, cast off the dregs, and digest that which will build blood and bone. The blood and bone that will make her a unique and "well made" person with a mind as individual as her fingerprints.

I doubt that any school wants to produce clones. I sincerely hope not. I trust that schools and educators want to forge unique and sentient individuals who think for themselves and who do not always fall into line. Nonconformity is a precondition for all good thinking, good art, and good science. This is one of the first lessons that a study of art and history teaches us.

No matter whether a kid wants to be an executive, a writer, a scientist, or a farmer he must learn to try to think and be what he wants to think and be. Not what his parents want him to think or be. Not what his teachers want him to think or be. Not what his priests and ministers want him to think or be. And certainly not what his sweetie wants him to think or be—art teaches us this.

And it teaches us that we must persist in the face of failure. Not to fail is to be perfect. William Faulkner said that his best work was that which failed the most and caused him the most trouble. He said that if he did something perfectly, "nothing would remain but to cut the throat and quit." This is why the novelist writes the next novel and why the painter paints the next painting.

And the novels and paintings which are enduring and aesthetically interesting, those novels and paintings we call art, stem from a common source, what Faulkner called "the travail of man within his environment, with his fellows, and with himself…"

And finally, let me point out that art, like medicine, the law, or gymnastics, demands a great deal from those who would be practitioners. Artists thrive on work, not on inspiration. Mozart is said to have observed that inspiration is always *ex post facto*; Faulkner allowed that he knew all about inspiration, saying that it always came at eight o'clock in the morning.

Art, like all great endeavors, requires only that the petitioner be devoted, determined, and bear a modest aptitude. Melville said that nothing "can take the place of persistence. Talent will not. Nothing is more unsuccessful than common men with talent. Genius will not. Unrewarded genius is almost a proverb. Education will not. The world is full of uneducated derelicts. Persistence and determination alone are omniscient."

Could more important lessons be learned from any subject?

REGARDING NORMAN ROCKWELL

Art hath no enemy but ignorance. —*John Taylor*

PAINTING SHOULD BE ENJOYED for its own sake, just as music is enjoyed—the pure delight of sounds moving in rhythm and space. We don't need to see a river to enjoy Bedřich Smetana's *The Moldau*, nor an image of an empty tomb to thrill, over and over again, to George Frederic Handel's *Hallelujah Chorus*. By the same token, we do not need a representative element to enjoy or thrill to a painting. We should, as Whistler said, be able to enjoy a work of art for what it is—paint, line, shape, contrast, color, and so on—not confusing painting with things that are "entirely foreign to it, like love, patriotism, and the like."

What is of preeminent value in any painting is the painter's expertise in managing the interplay of visual elements in his or her compositions with the physical materials and techniques of the chosen medium. If this is poorly done, no amount of narrative content can elevate the painting much above Elvis on black velvet.

You may remember the big stink that erupted at Congressional levels a few years ago over the 1987 photograph by Andres Serrano called *Piss Christ*—an object Jesse Helms, the Christian Coalition, and the new Newtonians would have the American people think was funded with federal money when it wasn't. It was the exhibit the picture was displayed in that was funded with federal money.

To me, *Piss Christ* is an innocuous image, much more so than, say, his very moving *The Morgue* pictures. *Piss Christ* is an image is of a plastic and wood crucifix suspended in a reddish-amber liquid medium with bubbles floating all about it. If it were not for the title, which is the only way one could identify the reddish-amber liquid as urine (and who knows if it really is?), no one would object to it. In fact, few would probably pay much attention to it at all. It is the outrageousness of the title of the picture that Serrano depends on for his impact, not the outrageousness of the image.

Ok. So where is this leading me?

To an epiphany I had in a dentist's office in 1967 in Easthampton, Massachusetts. My little family and I had just moved here from Tennessee and I probably had a few cavities from eating all them grits, hushpuppies, and pecan pies. I was sitting and waiting for my turn in the chair and was reading an old and doggy *Look* magazine. I turned a page and was bowled over by a picture. It was highly abstract and for a moment I thought it was a painting by Franz Kline. But I looked closer and read the caption: *The Problem We All Live With* by Norman Rockwell.

Well shut my mouth.

Like most fine art students in the 60s, my beginnings were overshadowed by the powerful figures of the then-dominant and fashionable Academy, Abstract Expressionism—Franz Kline, Mark Rothko, Adolph Gottlieb, Jackson Pollock. Great painters, all of them. But not Norman Rockwell; his work was not worthy of my serious attention. He was merely an "illustrator."

But what happened there in the dentist's office was that I had gotten hold of a copy of *Look* magazine that had made a bad trip through the printing press and was seriously out of register. The subject matter of the painting had been obscured beyond recognition, and I was forced to confront the painting on its purely formal terms as Clive Bell and James Whistler admonish us to do.

And it seriously passed muster.

It forced me, if I were to have an ounce of intellectual integrity and honesty about me, to reassess my position—my prejudice—regarding Norman Rockwell.

No one can fault Mr. Rockwell for any lack of quality in his work. His skill is, for me, a welcome antidote in a time when technique and craftsmanship have fallen into the wallow of disrepair.

REGARDING CHILDREN'S BOOKS, SEX & VIOLENCE

JOHN GARDNER, writing in the *Art of Fiction*, cautioned writers to avoid the cute, the corny, and the obvious. This advice is no less germane to painters or to middle-aged illustrators. But it is good advice that unfortunately goes unheeded by many editors, publishers, and illustrators of children's books. There is a veritable *bête noire* of cute on the shelves of children's bookstores and libraries. A canker of cornpone. An emetic of the obvious.

When I work for a juvenile audience I try to never be cute, corny, or obvious, though I do tend to amuse children with my illustrations, whereas with adults I tend to shock. (I think it was Mae West who said that the purpose of art is not to entertain but to disturb—and if she said it, she was right.)

When I work for a young audience I look for humor and surprise. I suppose that's because I'd rather see a child laugh than cry, and because many of the texts offered to me are themselves humorous.

In general, I avoid violent images because television, movies, and video games bombard kids with too much violence, and I do not need, nor want to countenance it in my own work.

This is not to say, however, that if an act of violence or a violent image were central to a story I would shy away from it. I would not, unless my editor pulled rank and forced me to. In fact, of the four stories I have written for children, three of them have some fairly violent moments. To shy away from the difficult and disturbing, *per se*, is to talk down to children, to treat them as intellectual inferiors, and I think this is a great mistake. Ernest Hemingway said that the best piece of equipment a writer can have is a "built-in shock-proof shit-detector." Well let me tell you, children have the best ones on the market. They can smell insincerity, condescension, and dishonesty a mile away. So could we all at one time or another in our lives. It's unfortunate that we let half-assed educators, the media, politicians, and Madison Avenue convince us that they know better.

Likewise, I and many other children's book illustrators tend to avoid sexual images, even something as innately benign as nudity. And this is a frustrating issue for me. I am not sure why we avoid it, nor am I at all convinced that we should.

An example.

Years ago, when my youngest daughter Madeline was five or six years old, I took her to see a film called *Coming Home* starring Jane Fonda, Bruce Dern, and Jon Voight. A good film. A good story. And there was a right steamy love scene with Fonda and Voight. As I handed our tickets to the young man who was taking them up, he stopped me and whispered close to my face, "Sir, do you realize that this is an R-rated movie?"

"Yes," I said, "Why?"

"Well sir, er ... uh ... you know," he said gesturing with his eyes and head toward Madeline, "the sex scene ... and ... and ... you know, the little one."

I ignored him, took Madeline by the hand, and went on in. We bought some popcorn and Raisinettes and enjoyed the picture show. But I kept brooding on what the boy had said. It bothered me because the week before I had taken Maddy to the same theater to see *The Dirty Dozen* starring Telly Savalas and a gang of other machos who, for the better part of two hours, went about blowing up the local terrain and each other. I have no idea how high the body count went in that picture, but it was certainly in the dozens if not hundreds. And, the ticket taker paid no attention to the little one that night. He did not question the wisdom of my letting Madeline see deceit and mayhem and war and murder and rape.

Jack Nicholson supposedly said, when defining the difference between an R-rated movie and an X-rated movie, "If you kiss a woman's breast you get an X. If you cut it off, you get an R."

Is something confused here?

Why is it that we link sex and violence? Is it that our not-yet post-puritan American society draws a parallel between the two?

REGARDING BAD LANGUAGE

I DO A LOT OF SPEECHES and lectures and I use vulgar language only if it is unavoidable or if it is dialectically or idiomatically useful. I never use inappropriate language, because all language is, by its very nature, appropriate. Language is the most human of all things human, and is therefore capable of expressing both the basest and noblest of human thoughts, ideas, and impulses.

Besides, my Mamma told me that it was impolite to use bad language in public, and most southerners try to be, if nothing else, polite.

Yet in my family there was some pretty bad language used, especially when the men fished, or pitched horseshoes, or argued politics. And I love them for it. I owe them a debt because it was that rough and imperfect language with its comfortable cadences, fractured syntax, and punctuations of Pig-Latin and profanity that inculcated in me an early love of language—not a love of nouns and pronouns, or adverbs and adjectives, but a love of the rhythm and play of words.

The women in my family were somewhat more demure in their speech than the men, though not by much. This was especially noticeable in front of preachers or Christian Science practitioners. For instance, my mother said swan, instead of "swear," as in "Well, I swan." She was euphemistic about stronger words too, saying "Shoot!" instead of its alliterative cousin.

Although I am now a born-again Yankee and have lived among Yankees for 28 years, I have come to the conclusion that southerners, who sometimes "egg each other on" and "get each other's goat," many of whom "ain't fit to roll with the pigs," who "crack doors," "mash" buttons, "cook on the front burner," "buy pigs in pokes," get "thangs outta horses' mouths," "whip the devil around stumps," then "root hog or die," do indeed have a more colorful language than New Englanders, despite the fact that my assistant, Kate Kiesler, a Vermont Yankee from Stowe, once described rained-on ice as being slicker than snot on a doorknob.

Mother's best friend was a woman named Vernita Gholston. They lived across the street from each other all their lives. Vernita held Mother in her arms and comforted her the day my young father was buried, and then helped her raise her two babies. My mother was "Billie" to Vernita when they were alone, and "Miss Wilhelmina" when they weren't. Mother called Vernita a "negress." Everybody else called her a nigger.

Now there's a bad word for you.

And what makes it bad is not its consanguinity with God, sex, or scat—the most common attributes of so-called bad words—but rather its consanguinity with fear, dogma, ignorance, and arrogance.

Standing ankle deep in a pond near a Nazi death camp in Poland, the British scientist and philosopher Jacob Bronowski gestured to the nearby buildings and said: "This is the concentration camp and crematorium at Auschwitz.… Into this pond were flushed the ashes of some four million people. And that was not done by gas. It was done by arrogance. It was done by dogma. It was done by ignorance. When people believe that they have absolute knowledge, … this is how they behave. This is what men do when they aspire to the knowledge of gods." (Or when they are certain that they have God on their side, know his will, and believe without doubt or question that they are RIGHT).

I come from several generations of racists and bigots. I am myself a recovering racist. My grandfather was a Klansman, as was his son, my uncle

Floyd, who worked shotgun on a chain gang in Hamilton County, Tennessee. My cousin Wayland knows, without a doubt, that only Southern Baptists are going to pass through the pearly gates of Paradise. Others of my family are certain that he's wrong. They know that only members of The Church of the Nazarene are going to heaven. Cath'lics don't stand a chance. Jews never did.

Of course you realize that racism and bigotry are not unique to Dixie. Here in the Commonwealth of Massachusetts we have home-grown Neo-Nazis and Skinheads. The Ku Klux Klan is active in Connecticut, as it is in New York and New Jersey. In 1993 two teen-aged Skinheads murdered their parents and younger brother for being "race traitors." And this happened in Pennsylvania, not Mississippi. According to The Southern Poverty Law Center in Montgomery, Alabama, there are nearly five hundred organized hate groups in America, and this does not include any of the militias we have read about. Only six states reported no hate crimes or organizations in 1994.*

So, having descended (or ascended, if you will) from this kind of background, I think I can say with some authority that my family's racism and bigotry were tethered not only to the ignorance, arrogance, and dogma that Jacob Bronowski speaks of, but were also tethered to fear. Blind, white fear. Fear that their place in society was being usurped. Fear that their values were under attack by unseen, sinister forces. Fear that their way of life was being challenged and questioned and that there was nothing they could do about it. Fear that all those people about whom my aunt Velma said, "You know, honey, those people just aren't like us," might actually have been very much like us, if only we had looked with an open heart and an open mind — but we didn't.

---

* As reported in *Harper's Magazine*, March 2000, p. 96.

Shadow Plays in Black & White

A Comparison of Dorothy and Alice

An Address to the Lewis Carroll Society
Boston Public Library, November 15, 1986

I FIRST CAME TO *The Wonderful Wizard of Oz* in 1982. I had never read any of L. Frank Baum's work before. In fact, I can't remember ever having seen the Judy Garland movie all the way through. But it was late December and I was in St. Martin with my three daughters for a winter vacation. One afternoon, I was sitting on the beach as a terrific storm was brewing on the horizon. The sky was very gray, and the clouds rolled fiercely towards our villa. I love storms and just sat there, watching the clouds approach. Now, you have to understand that I'm not given to hearing voices or seeing visions—and it was much too early in the day for me to have been drinking—nevertheless, on that stormy winter day, I saw a vision: a face in the rolling, gray storm clouds. The face of my old friend Gordon Cronin, a bookseller who, at the time, was married to my ex-wife. As you can imagine, I'm certainly not given to thinking about Gordon while relaxing, but there it was, his rotund face up there in the turbulent clouds. And THAT'S when it came to me: a logical follow-up to the Alice books could be *The Wizard of Oz*. I didn't even know the correct title of Baum's text, but since both were stories about little girls who get to their respective wonderlands by way of funnel-shaped insinuations, I imagined that I'd be able to make a case for doing an American Alice—Dorothy from Kansas. Whether or not my case for this American Alice would work on a scholarly or critical level would remain a mystery until I was able to find the text and read it.

When I got home, I contacted Justin Schiller, a devoted Ozmaniac and scholar and queried him about my hunch. He encouraged me to continue, so I bought a copy of *The Wonderful Wizard of Oz* and read it. Mind you, I was not taken by the Denslow pictures, nor was I particularly impressed with Baum's prose, but I was struck by the parallels that I perceived between the stories of the two little girls.

I know that Baum had read *Alice*, because he wrote in *The Advance* (August 19, 1909) that the "secret of *Alice*'s success lay in the fact that she was a real child," one that "any normal child could sympathize with." Her story, he said, "may often bewilder the little one—for it is bound to bewilder us, having neither plot nor motive in its relation—but Alice is doing something every moment, and doing something strange and marvelous, too; so the child follows her with rapturous delight. It is said that Mr. Dodgson, the author, was so ashamed that he had written a child's book that he could only allow it to be published under the pen name of Lewis Carroll; but it made him famous, even then, and 'Alice in Wonderland,' [*sic*] rambling and incoherent as it is, is one of the best and perhaps the most famous of modern fairy tales."

Finding this critique established for me the premise that Baum had most likely been influenced by Carroll in creating Dorothy. I have no idea if Baum was conscious of this or not, or, indeed, if it ever occurred to him. Probably not. But that didn't mean it wasn't right. I thought it valid to assume the parallel between Alice and Dorothy and to that premise, I made a commitment. This commitment took form in both obvious and subtle manifestations, which we will look at more closely.

Let's start with the heroines.

Dorothy, Frank Baum said in *The Emerald City of Oz*, was "like dozens of little girls you know. She was loving and usually sweet-tempered, and had a round rosy face and earnest eyes. Life was a serious thing to Dorothy, and a wonderful thing too, for she had encountered more strange adventures in her short life than many other girls her age."

Similarly, in April, 1887, Lewis Carroll wrote an article for *The Theatre* called "Alice on Stage" in which he asked "What wert thou, dream-Alice, in thy foster father's eyes? Loving, first, loving and gentle: loving as a dog (forgive the prosaic simile, but I know no earthly love so pure and perfect), and gentle as a fawn: then courteous—courteous to all, high or low, grand or grotesque, King or Caterpillar, even as though she were herself a King's daughter, and her clothing of wrought gold: then trustful, ready to accept the wildest possibilities with all that utter trust that only dreamers know; and lastly curious, and with the eager enjoyment of Life that comes only in the happy hours of childhood, when all is new and fair, and when Sin and Sorrow are but names—empty words signifying nothing!"

From their foster fathers' descriptions, one sparse and Yankee-like, the other florid and luxurious, it might seem that two very different little girls were being described. The language itself gives this impression. But when the descriptions are read carefully, the little girls are revealed to be quite similar: both are courteous and kind, gentle and sweet-tempered. And beyond the descriptions, we know that both Dorothy and Alice were products of the nineteenth century Anglo societies; they were born into male-dominated societies; they both embarked accidentally on a solitary voyage; and (not insignificantly) they both enjoyed the companionship of pets.

I took those similarities and created a kind of visual connection between my own versions of these stories by using the same model for the illustrations of both little girls. As you know, Carroll had originally illustrated the story himself in its holograph form, which was called *Alice's Adventures*

Underground. His model was Alice Liddell, and, I am sorry to say, the portrait is very clumsily drawn. However, as if to assure the recipient of the manuscript that it was indeed her own dark-eyed, dark-haired self that he intended the reader to see while reading the story, he pasted in a small, trimmed down photograph of the real Alice as a *cul-de-lampe*. Let there be no mistake, it was Alice Liddell to whom Lewis Carroll told the story on that June afternoon, and whom he saw in his mind's eye as he wrote the story down albeit to assuage her persistent nagging.

That Carroll's original Alice was dark-eyed and brunette prompted my first departure from the usual portraits of a blond haired and blue-eyed Alice. My model for my Alice was my youngest daughter, Madeline Nell, at age ten, who, at that point in her life, bore an uncanny and remarkable resemblance to Alice Liddell at the same age—especially as we see her in the eros-charged photograph Dodgson made of her as a little beggar girl. I simply followed Carroll's lead, using the spitting image döppelganger of Alice Liddell in the form of my Madeline.

It also followed when I committed to designing and illustrating the Baum book that I used Madeline as my model for Dorothy as well. Not because she had a "round rosy face and earnest eyes" as Baum noted, but because her physiognomy paralleled that of Alice Liddell—and I saw Alice and Dorothy as a kind of English and American version of each other (plates 11 & 12).

Now let us consider other intriguing similarities between the two tales.

As I mentioned in the beginning, each girl begins her journey, her voyage solitaire, if you will, by way of a cone-shaped hole. One girl falls down a rabbit hole into a Wonderland thinking, as she tumbles through space, about her tabby cat Dinah—wondering if cats eat bats or bats eat cats. The other girl falls *up* a hole, a cyclone, into the Land of Oz with her little dog, Toto, tagging along with her.

If we think about it, we can see that the voyages themselves reflect the contrasting landscapes in which Alice and Dorothy live. Dorothy lives on the open prairie. Alice lives on an island. Open spaces as opposed to insular spaces. I might also suggest agoraphobic space, as opposed to claustrophobic space, if one accepts, as I do, that these two "dream" stories are more nightmare than whimsy. I played with this idea in my treatments of the tales not only with the images but with the design and typography.

Look at the image of the Queen of Hearts' Rose Garden, for instance. We know that the door into the garden is very small. Alice had to nibble on a bit of that funky mushroom she kept in her pocket to get herself down-sized enough to get through the door. Once through the door she sees, according to Carroll, the garden, which is full of bright flower beds and cool fountains. According to Moser it is also full of fanciful topiaries, sun-dials, astrolabes, birdbaths with grotesque ornaments, and a ceiling. A ceil-ing like one might find in a flat-roofed greenhouse. Closed space, but in the sense of mirrors, infinite. Compare that to my image of the prairie when Dorothy has returned home: a tiny farmhouse and windmill on a sea of grass. Infinite, open space contained only by her memories and dreams.

And look at the bindings: *Alice* and *Looking-Glass* are half-leather: leather spine and full-length leather fore-edge. The panel in between is, in the case of *Alice*, marble paper that my daughter Cara and I made at Gray Parrot's workshop, and in the case of *Looking Glass*, it is printed paper. The overall effect is rich and elegant, befitting a child of Victorian wealth and privilege. The binding for *Oz*, designed by David Bourbeau and myself, is, by contrast, open. We used Barcham Green watercolor paper over boards with a simple gold stamping on the front panel and a blind stamp on the back panel. It evokes a feeling of spaciousness and humility. No tooled leather and marbled paper for this child of poverty, this child of the prairies, this child of dust.

The typographic conceits also allude to this agro-claustro-effect. The typography for the Alice books is a long page set unjustified on a narrow measure. The chapters run on, with the heads printed in Oxford blue. The text block is bounded by extremely wide margins, which form the play-ground for red shoulder notes that are always justified towards the gutter. They frame and close in the text. Some of the shoulder notes are illustrated, others are not. Some are long. Some are short. All in all, the effect of the typography is, I hope, one of decorated and calculated pandemonium.

By contrast, the design and typography of *Oz* is simple and based on the word OZ. The O, being as it is in classic forms very nearly an inscription of a square, informed the page size, 10 by 11 inches, or very nearly a square. The proportions of the Z, as drawn by the likes of Frederic Goudy and David Goines informed the proportions of the text block. The margins more or less follow the rules of the Golden Mean as defined by Jan Tschichold. All in all, the effect is one of simplicity and spaciousness which befits the design of a story that springs out of life on a dusty prairie farm. The chapters always open a new recto, which bears nothing but the chapter number and the chapter title. There is lots of white space in these chapter openings, especially since the facing verso is either short or nonexistent. The versos of the chapter heads are also blank except for the final image. The only decoration takes place in the form of colored running heads. The colors are based on the Map of the Marvelous Land of Oz that was drawn in 1914 by one Professor Wogglebug (which was Frank Baum himself, of course). The reader can tell where in the Land of Oz he or she is by the color of the running heads. (I might note that the land of the Wicked Witch is yellow, a wretched typographic color, and that the yellow brightens somewhat after the witch's meltdown.)

In his introductory note to *The Wonderful Wizard of Oz*, Frank Baum said that the "old-time fairy tale, having served for generations, may now be classed as 'historical' in the children's library; for the time has come for a series of newer 'wonder-tales' in which the stereotyped genie, dwarf and fairy are eliminated, together with all the horrible and blood-curdling incident devised by their authors to point a fearsome moral to each tale. Modern education includes morality; therefore the modern child seeks only entertainment in its wonder tales and gladly dispenses with all disagreeable incident.

"Having this thought in mind, the story of 'The Wonderful Wizard of Oz' was written solely to pleasure children of today. It aspires to being a modernized fairy-tale, in which the wonderment and joy are retained and the heartaches and nightmares are left out."

Now, who is this guy kidding? No nightmares in the *Wizard of Oz*? I would like to hear him explain the decapitation of the wild cat, or the confrontation by the terrible kalidah. How about that wolf pack? The wood of fighting trees? The spider monster? The hammerheads?

Likewise, the Alice books abound in monsters and weirdos. Remember the enormous puppy? The Jabberwock? The March Hare and the Mad Hatter? The banquet for Queen Alice?

All three books are populated by large, overbearing, and largely impotent males: the Guardian of the Gate to the Emerald City; the soldier with the green whiskers; the cracked-in-the-head Mr. Joker (based on Jerry Falwell who carries a marotte in the guise of George Bush); the not-so-wizardly Wizard himself (based not on Jack Nicholson or John Gielgud as some have suggested [Julia Bristow, *Virginia Pilot and Ledger Star*, August 24, 1986], but on Ronald Reagan, a wizard if ever there was one—who else could make something out of nothing?) Consider the addled, hen-pecked King of Hearts who keeps his hat on with hat pins to the head. What of the three-inch caterpillar? The brothers Tweedle—Dee and Dum? The clumsy Red Knight and the poor, hapless White Knight who bears an unmistakable resemblance to Charles Dodgson. And the most famous of them all— the cowardly lion, the tin man, and the scarecrow.

The impotent male figures are, however, more than offset by the presence of dominant and threatening female figures: the Duchess and her pepper box; the Queen of Hearts with her decapitation fixation; the nasty, hairy-chinned Red Queen (based on my friend and colleague Jane Yolen, who sat dutifully and willingly for an unflattering portrayal); the witch of the North (based on my college-days house-mother, Lillian Carter, President Carter's mother), and the wicked witch of the West (who has been correctly suspected of having been based on Nancy Reagan). Now *there's* a literary character who's never ever given a single child any heartaches or nightmares.

And need I remind you that both girls encounter weird and strange apparitions? Dorothy encounters the Wizard in three ghostly guises: as the terrible beast, as the lovely lady, and as, yes, a disembodied head, which bears a striking resemblance to the CEO of a large automobile industry. Alice meets the Cheshire cat with his many very sharp teeth (unlike the keyboard-faced cat the Disney studios gave us). In my treatment the Cheshire Cat wisps and smiles in a tree on the outskirts of an Anglican cemetery, my nod to the theme of death that Carroll introduces as Alice falls though the rabbit hole. I will come back to this momentarily.

And what of potions? There is a little bit of the rhizotomist in both texts: the little vial which has a beautifully printed label that tells Alice, "Drink Me;" the little cake that commands her in currants to "Eat Me;" and that funky mushroom that she keeps in her pocket.

The Wizard makes up some heady potions too, doesn't he? He pours courage for the Lion out of a green bottle (I wonder if it is purely coincidental that the British call gin "Dutch Courage" and that Dutch gin comes in green bottles). He makes a silk and sawdust heart to fill a void in the chest of the tin Woodman. He put together bran and pins to make brains for the Scarecrow. It is not a stretch to imagine that a man who was capable of coming up with the word OZ by either advancing the initials of New York one letter each in the alphabet or who noticed that the second drawer in a file cabinet read O to Z could have dropped the final letter N off the word BRAN and the initial letter P off of the word PINS to arrive at BRAINS. An observation a little more interesting, I think, than the idea that the pins simply made him "sharp," as some observers have advanced.

In *The Robber Bridegroom*, Eudora Welty notes that "A journey is forever lonely and parallel to death." How true this is for our two young heroines. Both Dorothy and Alice think of death as they begin their journey. In the whirling wind of the cyclone Dorothy wonders if she will be "dashed to pieces" when the house falls again to the gray prairie ground. Similarly, as Alice is free-falling down the rabbit hole she finds an empty jar of orange marmalade and frets about dropping it "for fear of killing somebody." As my collaborator James Kincaid observed, this "is the first of a surprising number of references to death. The prominence of death, particularly as it is understood by Alice, is suggestive of one adult ordering system: death appears as a consequence of insisting on linear developments, endings." Death presages the feeling of loneliness which, to me, permeates all three stories. After all, both girls wanted nothing more than to get back home. Along the way they are given direction in the form of written signs: the signposts directing Alice to the Tweedle houses and the chalkboard insisting that Dorothy be allowed to go the Emerald City.

Some of the details and way stations of the voyages also bear comparison: the Gate to the Emerald City and the looking-glass, which has the vertical aspect of a door, or the door to the garden, or perhaps the door to Queen Alice's banquet. The wall of the Dainty China Country and Humpty-Dumpty's wall. The Scarecrow in the river and the riverbank of the Sheep Queen. The Wood of No Names and the Dismal Landscape. The Munchkin landscape and the wood of the wasp in a wig.

Consider too that both girls find crowns on their voyages. Dorothy's comes to her in the form of a golden cap she finds in the witch's cupboard. Alice gets hers when the white pawn moves to the Queen's eighth.

Another parallel is so obvious I probably ought not remark on it. But I think it's fun, so let's do it. Remember all the creatures that the girls encounter? The ones that fly, like the Jabberwock and the gryphon? The elephant bee and the bread-and-butter-fly? The winged monkeys? Which, by the way, in my reading are not winged in the usual sense of being winged, as with birds and angels, but winged in terms of a pilot getting his "wings" after learning to handle a flying machine. My flying monkeys have less to do with Jack Dawn's flying monkeys in the movie than with Leonardo's ornithopter, a Rube Goldberg sort of contraption that runs, as I designed it, on methane gas (plate 13).

And what about the creatures the girls encounter that don't fly? Like the mouse in the pool of tears, the pig baby, the hedgehog, the dodo, the dandy horse in the carriage, the sartorial white rabbit, the dormouse and the Queen of the field mice?

And the flowers: remember the talking rose, the tiger lilies, the field of deadly poppies.

Ben Shahn, in *The Shape of Content*, tells the young artist to read everything but the critics. I think that is good advice, though I do not necessarily follow it myself. I read them and take what they say with a grain of salt, believing with Rilke that art is of such stuff as to be little touched by criticism. Occasionally, however, I read a review of my own work that does touch me. Touches me because the critic finds in my work attributes that I had overlooked. Makes me see things that I hadn't noticed before. Things I wanted to see. Things I should have seen.

In a *Chicago Tribune* review of my edition of *The Wonderful Wizard of Oz* (August 3, 1986), Paul Skenazy did just that. He noted that my pictures "sharpen the contrast between the realistic and fantastic aspects of Wonderland, allowing one to appreciate more fully how Baum has mediated memory with fantasy. The illustrations also sadden (as they naturalize) the story, urging us out of our suspension of disbelief. Entrancing and gloomy, gorgeous and tender, Moser's *Oz* is no longer the optimistic turn-of-the-century romp that Baum and Denslow hoped to create, but an end-of-the-century retrospective, drawn less for the ageless imagination of children than for the aging temper of adults solemnly looking back to adventures remembered with an ashen strain of loss and regret."

Skenazy also saw quite clearly that color has always been critical to the spell of *Oz*—whether one remembers the Denslow illustrations or the 1939 film. "But all that has changed" he notes, because "Moser and his Pennyroyal Press, known for coming up with startling new visions of old classics for some time [have created] a suspiciously adult reading of Baum's homely tale … [an] entire volume … in paler shades of gray, a shadow play in black and white."

Forty-Seven Days to Oz

The following account of the process of inventing the sixty-two images for L. Frank Baum's *The Wonderful Wizard of Oz* was taken directly from the day book that I keep to chronicle my work. Entries are made daily for the most part, usually at night, and usually after the day's work is done and my brain has been treated to a bit of gin or bourbon. Made hurriedly, there is little thought given to syntax and composition. Therefore, I have done some rudimentary editing for the sake of clarity and to repair injuries done to the language. Care has been taken, however, to reflect the hurried flavor of the language and the informal mood of the day book.

It is misleading to suggest that the images for the Pennyroyal *Oz* were accomplished in only forty-seven days. While it is true that the one hundred and thirty-five preparatory studies were indeed executed in forty-seven days, it should be noted that nearly two years of meditation, conversation, and research had been done before I commenced the drawings.

APRIL 1, 1985   ℭ After rest and relaxation, I begin, in earnest, my work on the *Oz*: I am reminded of hearing M. F. K. Fisher saying on NPR that "all day long I play music, I clean out drawers. I don't read much. I write a little, I drift about. I await the next day." ℭ Reread the notes I've been gathering for the past eighteen months. Made the drawing for the cyclone.

APRIL 2, 1985, 5 A.M.   ℭ Began drawings of the Prairie Landscape. Dorothy is a simple small silhouetted figure—no interest (at this point) in her appearance—only her impression. The windmill in the distance anticipates machinery. The mail boxes suggest remove, distance, far away places. As the text dictates, there are no trees or houses. Dorothy is the solitary voyager. ℭ The Family Portrait relies heavily upon the WPA photos of Walker Evans & Ben Shahn—echoing the current plight of farmers in the U.S. (Reagan recently suggested that farmers be exported and that we keep the grain. The farmers responded that they would be glad to do so if they could take some of their grain with them to show the world that Americans could make something other than bombs.) Dorothy's face echoes Alice's face—a subtle but conscious effort to parallel and contrast the Alice books & *Oz*. She is set apart from Uncle Henry and Aunt Em by the post and is seen against the interior of the house (where her *voyage solitaire* begins) and against a window suggesting escape and light.

APRIL 3, 1985, 5:22 A.M.   ℭ The drawing for the Chalk Board done. Drawing done for Home Again—Here I use the house, newly built, suggesting warmth & familiarity in contrast to the prairie landscape which is stark and lonely. The sky will be a montage of the characters Dorothy has met as I did in "The Reverie of Alice's Sister." The gray of this print will be warmer than the gray of the prairie landscape.

APRIL 4, 1985, 5:30 A.M.   ℭ Began and finished drawing for the Landscape of the Munchkins. I have in mind Rousseau & Church—particularly Church's Jamaican sketches—as well as my own travels to Barbados, Tortola, and Jost Van Dyke. The landscapes throughout will stress the ambiguities and non sequiturs of the Caribbean, Eastern forests, and the Kansas farmland. ⟨ 11:05 a.m. BOQ: since there is no mention of midgets or achondroplasia in the text I use the precision of Baum's text to establish the scale of a Munchkin: the hat, which we are told is "twelve inches" high. Recognizing Baum's interest in costume, I use rural American costume allowing the ambiguities existing to suggest "odd" elements. The model is Frank Tengle, a sharecropper from Alabama photographed by Walker Evans.

APRIL 5, 1985 3:15 P.M.   ⟨ Drawing done of the Witch of the North. ⟨ Began the yellow brick road sequence and ran into serious constipation. Several hours of sketching and staring out my window. Got away for a while, came back to it and finished a drawing for the Yellow Brick Road. I have doubts, but will rest on it and start up afresh tomorrow. At this point I'm questioning the rigidity of the format—considering images of different sizes.

APRIL 6, 1985   ⟨ Drawing prepared for the Mouse Queen—though there is no mention of costume—in fact, she evidently cannot be told from any other mouse (according to the Woodsman). I have opted, as did Dens-low, for costume. (N. B. See entry dated 12 April).

APRIL 7, 1985   ⟨ Have come to the conclusion that neither my fingers nor my mind have yet found the pulse of Oz.

APRIL 8, 1985   ⟨ Having meditated on the problem overnight, I became more and more convinced that the images have to be smaller, they need to have a lot of space around them—after all, the whole story is a contrast between the openness of Kansas prairies, and the insular, land bound, and claustrophobic land of Oz. Small things should be pictured small.   ⟨ All day I played with different shapes for the pictures and I know I've made the appropriate decision. For the first time I feel that I've found the pulse of the scheme and it quickens my own pulse. Before, it was far too pedestrian but now wonderful abstract juxtapositionings are possible. It breathes.   ⟨ Dinner with Jeff Dwyer and Paul Mariani—Steven Schoenberg unable to join us as planned, due to a bad sore throat. After dinner, drank (pleasantly, not sloppily,) paced out the entire book. Quit at 2:30 a.m. Will look at it afresh in the morning.

APRIL 9, 1985   ℂ Finding the cadence is the most important thing right now (as it is with every book) and that it was improper, faulty cadence that was giving me pause all last week. Spent the day with my camera and car, wandering around the nearby landscape, looking for things.

APRIL 11, 1985   ℂ Part of the problem of beginning the *Oz* images lay in my being far too precious about the drawings—seeing them as exhibit pieces rather than as vehicles of thought and development. Hence, today I made drawings for the Lion, the Yellow Brick Road, Scarecrow in the Cornfield. (I redrew the Witch of the North, after discovering that I had not adequately read the text—the Witch of the North wears a pointed hat and is covered with stars.) Drawing should properly be responsive and meditative, not studied and contrived.

APRIL 12, 1985, 6 A.M.   ℂ Began and finished the study for the Stork. I find that I have to move rapidly. If I slow down to make notes, to reflect on what I'm doing while I'm doing it, the process becomes terribly constricting. Images spring more keenly from the hand and eye than from the mind. Up to this point the mind has been in control of this project and now must give way to eye & hands.   ℂ Drawings completed for the Mouse Queen (after having deferred to the accuracy of the text & left her unidentifiable), The Deadly Field of Poppies, and the decapitated head of the Wild Cat—Baum insists his story is without nightmares, but I don't really think so.

APRIL 13, 1985, 8 A.M.   ℂ Did the preliminary drawings for the Guardian of the Gate using Edwin Meese as the model. Omby Amby study finished, using Alexander Haig as the model.

APRIL 14, 1985   ℂ Awoke feeling that neither the drawing nor the politics were right for the Guardian of the Gate. Resolved to redo it and did so using Cap Weinberger as the model, sporting (as does Omby Amby) a rather Germanic costume, and brandishing (while asleep) a rather ridiculous weapon (a 16th-century Italian rifle with war hammer).   ℂ Began drawings for the four faces of Oz.

APRIL 15, 1985   ℂ After toying with the faces of Jerry Falwell, Jim Bakker, Jimmy Swaggart, and Oral Roberts, I came to the decision that a symbol of American corporate power rather than the radical right-wing televangelists were more properly apropos to the image of Oz as the Great Head, the first spokesman for the Wizard. Who else could better be that symbol than Lee Iacocca? America today exists for and makes policies for corporations (Central America, South Africa) rather than for her people.   ℂ The Ball of Fire I will steal from *Paradiso*.   ℂ The Oz as the Lovely Lady: using Jeanne Kirkpatrick as a model—one can assume that since Scarecrow has no brains he might conceivably think her "a lovely creature." Other options are Rita Lavelle, Maureen Reagan, and Anne Burford. "I never grant favors without some return." says the Lovely Lady.   ℂ The Oz as the Most Terrible Beast: "A more dreadful monster could not be imagined"—and such a monster is the CIA. Therefore William Casey gives me the nose, mouth and two of the monster's five eyes—one is very secret—covert, as it were. (N.B.: This drawing was later redrawn without human elements. See entry for 11 May) ℂ The Castle of the Witch of the West is taken from photographic studies of a castle I made in La Mancha, near Guadalerzas.

APRIL 16, 1985   ℂ Drawing done for the Wicked Witch of the West. I'm playing very close to obvious and corny imagery here using the large blacks, the pointed hat—but doing so intentionally.   ℂ Drawings also done for the Leader of the Wolves (a coyote) & the King of the Crows (a raven).

APRIL 17, 1985   ℂ Made the drawing for The Witch Liquidated.

APRIL 18, 1985 ❲ Made the drawing for Dorothy's Silver Shoes.

APRIL 19, 1985 ❲ As is so often the case, the simplest (and least important) images take the most time, thought, and energy. The Tin Woodsman's Axe, newly fitted with a golden handle and silver head (it must also bear Winkie magic, for surely without magic such a handle would bend). I approach the image at first from a purely inventive point of view. That yielded little good, so I covered an axe with tinfoil and photographed it. The camera was no help in this instance, so I simply made studies from the model—I think I sometimes jump too quickly for the camera. I trust that using the camera as I am doing is experimental for me and not a crutch.

APRIL 19 & 20, 1985 ❲ In NYC. Met my old teacher George Cress for dinner at Trastevere. Saturday morning photographed the lions in front of the New York Public Library. The Lion in Oz should properly be a library lion.

APRIL 21, 1985 ❲ Photographed in Childs Park, various local landscapes with weeping willows, the Smith College Greenhouses, and the lions at Wistariahurst. Have been fighting a terrible influenza for a week now—the worst of it is fatigue—I tire quickly & can't work as long—need more sleep. My brain is out of synchronization with all the rest. I can't even keep the days in the log correctly. Improving today.

APRIL 22, 1985 ❲ Went back to the Smith College greenhouses in the early morning to make more photographs. It becomes more and more apparent to me that all is a matter of thinking & rethinking & rethinking—of working & reworking & reworking—and of being not afraid to throw away work and ideas, no matter how long they've been worked at.

APRIL 23, 1985 ❲ The Dismal Landscape and the Gloomy Forest went without delay—using my own photos made on 9 April. ❲ Returned to the Smith Greenhouses for more photographs—I have been inspired there, and have found many things. Dinner with the kids and to a movie.

APRIL 24, 1985 ☙ Finished signing the 8500 prints for Bevis's Gold Rush. ☙ Drawings on blocks for the *Audubon Magazine* commission.

APRIL 25, 1985 ☙ Prepared the sketches for Sylvia Plath's *Above The Oxbow*. ☙ Signed the eight cases of books for the University of California Press. Interruptions to *Oz* are everywhere. Put off August vacation until September to give myself more time.

APRIL 28, 1985 ☙ With Madeline Moser to Nashville & Chattanooga.

APRIL 29, 1985 ☙ The problem now is the inability to concentrate. I want to work on nothing else but *Oz*. But work for the Audubon Society and the Plath project is immediate and pays the mortgages—so I do it to the detriment of *Oz*. So today (beyond a bit of *Oz* organization in the morning), I worked on the wood engraving *Forever & Ever Amen* for the Audubon Society. Dinner at Beardsley's with Stan Holwitz, Jeff Dwyer, and Elizabeth O'Grady.

APRIL 30, 1985 ☙ Finished engraving the two blocks for *Audubon Magazine*.

MAY 1, 1985 ☙ Reconciled all five panels of The Yellow Brick Road sequence.   ☙ Made the drawing for Lion Asleep on the Truck, based on the sleeping lion of Wistariahurst.   ☙ Made the study for a Kalidah.   ☙ In an article (*Time*, Jan. 31, 1983) Robert Hughes termed David Smith a *bricoleur*—one who uses up discarded things. My work is not dissimilar. I find myself more and more using and piecing together bumfodder.

MAY 2, 1985 ☙ Did the drawing for The Armed Winkies. The armor (one can, I think, assume that if the witch could/would give them sharp spears, she might as well give them armor) is invented as a hybrid of 17th-century Italian armor & bib overalls.   ☙ Drawing done for The Black Bees.

MAY 3, 1985 ☙ Finished the drawing for the King of the Flying Monkeys. Continuing my anachronistic play with costume & machinery, I have garbed him in leather flight helmet & jacket, aviator's white scarf (again playing close to the cusp of kitsch). His flying machine will belie him though. ℂ The Gate to the Emerald City is taken directly from my photographs of the huge circular boiler doors (manufactured by James Beggs & Co.) which were made for the Brassworks in Haydenville, Massachusetts. I reworked the monograms to read OZ, took off two of the existing handles, and added a combination lock. I am enjoying the immediacy of using the photo directly. Especially when one brings to it the wealth of drawing skills acquired over twenty-five years. There is also a viable implication of the use of machinery to produce these particular images.   ℂ Drawings done for Dorothy in the Golden Cap. Baum's images are sometimes so corny that it seems impossible to develop an image which isn't dumb and transparent. As I used my daughter Madeline as the model for Alice in *Alice's Adventures in Wonderland*, so I used her here as my model for Dorothy. The parallels between Alice & Dorothy are, I think, obvious. To begin with, Dorothy ascends up a funnel-shaped cloud. Alice descends a funnel-shaped hole. That opposite-yet-sameness pervades my thought—the sense of space (open vs. closed—American plains landscape vs. British landscape, etc., etc.). Her golden cap was the floppy crown made at Christmas for Harold P. McGrath by Elizabeth O'Grady and was pressed into service. [*Note:* this image was later completely redone, using Madeline Moser at age 13, in late July 1985]. ℂ Drawing done for The Gifts of the Winkies. Baum, as all Americans—no, most Americans—have a fixation with gold, silver, & precious jewels. ℂ Finished the day with the drawing of The Wizard Unmasked. Among my key thoughts are the Wizard's own words: "I have fooled everyone so long that I thought I should never be found out." "Here are the things I used to deceive you." "I am a Humbug." "You must keep my secret and tell no one that I am a humbug." "The people ... would be vexed with me for having deceived them." "I'm just a common man."

MAY 4, 1985   ℂ Yesterday finished with the first of several images of The Wizard Unmasked. Today I did a few more (plate 14), concentrating on an appropriate expression (aw-shucks didn't-mean-no-harm, coprophagous sort of expression). I am content with the child's sleeper costume adorned with stars & comets. ⊄ Discovered an old note to myself to refer to an image on p. 147 of the *Pictorial History of the American Circus*, a photograph of John Ringling, the youngest of the Ringling Brothers. Baum was fascinated by the Circus. The wizard worked for a circus as a barker. Reagan was an actor, a performer, a "ventriloquist," as it were. It all fits. I chose to make him very small on a large page, he is, after all, described by Dorothy as "a very little man." ⊄ Three studies done for the Humbug Wizard. Imagery which is too immediately recognizable will, I'm afraid, date the work— have to be careful.

MAY 5, 1985 ⊄ Drawing done for the Tin Woodsman's Heart. Toyed with the idea of a Jarvik heart but decided the liberty was too great and opted instead for the more correct (and corny) Dine-like heart.

MAY 6, 1985 ⊄ Most of the day spent working up the image of The Wizard Aloft. I began with news service photos of Reagan waving to crowds or giving his thumbs-up sign and built the balloon around him. The balloon is based on one from P. T. Barnum's Circus, in which his "professor Donaldson took off from Chicago in 1875 and never was seen again." Appropriate. ⊄ Dorothy, Distressed done from photos I made last summer on location for the filming of *Huck Finn*. ⊄ The Wood of the Fighting Trees I am using directly from photos I've made for this project—as indeed I am doing for all the landscapes. ⊄ Study for Glinda the Good finished, using daughter Cara as model.

MAY 7, 1985 ⊄ Day spent looking for things—pictures of Judy Garland & Jerry Falwell. Out in the late afternoon with the camera looking for the Wall to the Dainty China Country. ⊄ Set up and photographed still life studies for Scarecrow's Brains and Lion's Courage.

MAY 8, 1985 ⊄ Returned to the Brassworks in Haydenville to shoot the wall. Did drawing for The Delicate China Maid using Judy Garland as model (in her costume for her "*Oz*"). The use of Garland was originally Justin Schiller's idea, one which I liked then & now. It is appropriate on many levels—she herself was so very delicate &, perhaps more so than any book I've done, even *Frankenstein*, the *Oz* is associated with a film. An homage to that is not inappropriate. [*Note:* I later decided this was too much and used another, less familiar image of Miss Garland.]   ℭ First copies of *Huck Finn* back from the bindery. Lunch with Perry Smith in Keene, N.H.   ℭ Drawing done for Mr. Joker using Jerry Falwell as model—"he's a bit cracked." In his clasped, prayer-like hands he holds the joker's marotte, for which I used George Bush as the model (he has to be animated by somebody).

MAY 9, 1985   ℭ Back to Haydenville to catch the early morning light on the wall.   ℭ Did the drawing for The Peaceable Kingdom. Even though Baum mentions tigers, wolves, & foxes, I chose to use non-predatory animals and ones which a child would likely see in a circus. This conclusion I arrived at after considering using only native American animals. Began work on The Spider Monster—the enemy of the peaceable kingdom. I intended to use James Watt somehow, but will develop that idea for horror rather than parody.

MAY 10, 1985   ℭ I hope the reader will not immediately perceive the identities of these characters. After all, they are ideas, inferences, implications which I alone want to play with. They have nothing to do with the story Baum wrote nor any meanings or morals therein. Therefore, contrary to my original intention, there is no James Watt or Edward Teller in The Spider Monster—he became simply a giant, eight-eyed Wolf Spider.   ℭ The Quadling Farmer is a self-portrait as a circus dwarf. I felt I should have a dwarf somewhere in this work. First, because of their strong association with the circus (an atmosphere I'm trying to recall, if not evoke) and secondly, because dwarfs are expected in Oz—only I'm not using them where or how they are expected.

May 11, 1985   ℭ Drawing done for the Hammerhead—based on William Casey, who stands as a symbol for the CIA. Hammerheads are xenophobic, militaristic, and hide behind rocks. Their ability to extend their heads is for

me suggestive of a phallic motif which I have only hinted at.   ℭ Drawing
done for Lion's Courage. I have chosen to use, as the text dictates, a green
bottle of spirits. Gin. Dutch Gin. The British refer to gin as "Dutch Courage."
ℭ Drawing done for Scarecrow's Brains (plate 15) also done from photographs made in the studio on May 7. The conceit is that if the final letter
of Bran is dropped and the initial letter of Pins is likewise dropped, the con-
traction is quite simply "brains." There is evidence since Baum obviously
enjoyed such work/letter play (NY = OZ, e.g.) it seems entirely within reason that this might have been what he had in mind—not really "bran-new"
brains!

MAY 12, 1985   ℭ Relaxation with the family & a bit of tennis.

MAY 13, 1985   ℭ Off to NYC after morning meetings with JPD. Dinner
with Amanda Mackey, Mary Anne & Carolyn Hartwell.

MAY 14, 1985   ℭ In NYC with Casper Citron at the Algonquin, with
Pegeen Fitzgerald for WNCY NPR & with Don Swaid's *Book Beat* on
CBS radio. Home at 8 p.m. Shower, eat, & bed.

MAY 15, 1985   ℭ Drawing done for Scarecrow on the Pole in the River. ℭ
Drawing done for Toto, which may or may not be final—for certain it
won't be what is expected. Today it is a Skye Terrier, but soon it could be a
modified Jack Russell Terrier.   ℭ Drawing done for The Wall of the Dainty
China Country. Resisted the obvious pun on the Great Wall of China. The
drawing was based on photos made at the Brassworks in Haydenville on
May 9th.

MAY 16, 1985   ℭ Drawing for the Tin Woodsman prepared. I began with
the human figure and then "tinned" it and made it mechanical. This follows
the evolution of the Tin Woodsman as Baum gives it. It further reinforces
the interest in machinery that is manifested by Baum and his times.

MAY 17, 1985   ℂ The next to the final drawing is the Squadron of the Flying Monkeys. My initial impetus, following along the pattern of *fin de siècle* fascination with machinery, was to use either the early flying machines of Otto Lilienthal or our contemporary 'ultra-lights.' (The Wright brothers are in the correct period, and I found a trade name of "WIZARD" for an ultralight.) The mood of the modern machines is perhaps not quite right for Baum but the mechanics are. Further meditation and rereading of the text led me to abandon the machine as a fixed-wing craft. The flying monkeys arrive amid a lot of "chatter and fluttering of wings." This led me towards a Leonardo type machine, borne aloft (properly) by a balloon yet given flight by man- (monkey-) tailored wings. The balloon was forsaken for an on-board internal combustion engine which drives a propeller and something else, but god knows what. The craft is fitted out with pitot-tube, radar, radio, weather vane and arresting parachute.   ℂ Redrew the Cowardly Lion. ℂ Began the drawing of Scarecrow, Conversant. To set up and render, or to photograph a bag of hay with a hat takes only skill, but to invent a scarecrow's face, crudely drawn, takes naiveté. I have long since lost that naïveté. The drawing is suitable in all ways except for his features. I will have to enlist the aid of a child, I think. I will have to build him to photograph and redraw. (N. B. On July 27, with the aid of Susan Medlicott and my daughters, Madeline and Ramona, Scarecrow was built and taken into the Hatfield cornfields to be photographed. Madeline drew the face to insure a sense of graphic innocence). At 3:03 a.m. all the studies (135, in all) for the Oz are finished. Some revisions will undoubtedly be required. Forty-seven days it took to get to Oz.

THE WORKSHOP OF FILTHY CREATION

Illustrating FRANKENSTEIN

Was man, indeed, at once so powerful, so virtuous, and magnificent, yet so vicious and base? He appeared at one time a mere scion of the evil principle, and at another as all that can be conceived of noble and godlike. —Frankenstein's demon

WHEN I WAS A STUDENT at Auburn in 1958 I went to see the strippers at the county fair over in Opelika, Alabama with some of my fraternity brothers. "Granny Grundy and her Girls," I think the show was called. If not, it was something like that. I don't remember the girlie show, although I'm certain that we saw it because I remember the barker telling us to put our hands in our pockets and get a "good grip on life." There were freak shows, too, on the midway. A bunch of us went to see The Moon Man. He was a white man sitting in a circular pen-like affair. A raised walkway circumscribed it. He was wearing brown trousers and his socks were scrunched down above scruffy shoes. He sat on a bentwood chair, leaning forward and smoking a cigarette. Occasionally he looked up at us gawkers as we crowed and craned to have a look at him. His expression was detached. Nothing seemed to bother him, not even the taunts of Alabama rednecks and Auburn Kappa Alpha's. He just sat, smoking his cigarette, enduring or ignoring everything. The skin on his chest, shoulders, and back was flaky and rutted with deep pits which I am certain could be explained clinically as some sort of an exfoliative dermatitis or an *ichthyosis vulgaris* but to my freshman eyes it was just plain weird and disgusting. The effect was magnified by The Moon Man's casual, cigarette-smoking detachment from the spectators. But no matter how repulsive he was, I did not look away, except when his eyes caught mine.

I don't think that I am very much different from most people. All people, I think, have a fascination with the strange. An ambivalent attraction toward the repulsive.

David Lynch explored this brilliantly in his film about John Merrick, the Englishman who was known as "The Elephant Man." There are other stories equally as moving as Merrick's. I am thinking of Jo Jo the Dog-faced Man who went the rounds of the dime museums early in the century. His name was Fedor Jeftichew. His condition was hypertrichosis—an abnormal growth of hair where there should be none. A reporter for the *New York Herald Tribune* described his face as bearing a striking resemblance to a Skye terrier. And I am thinking of Julia Pastrana who was afflicted with the same or similar anomaly. A Mexican born in 1832, she stood only four feet high as an adult. Her face was pitifully misshapen and covered with shining black hair. She died at 28, shortly after giving birth to a baby that she hoped would be normal and would somehow vindicate her but instead turned out to be a dark little miniature of herself. It was said that she died of a broken heart.

There are hundreds of stories like these in the annals of carnival and circus history precisely because other "normal" people like to look and will pay money to do so with impunity.

When we are on a bus or a train or passing them on a street, it is more difficult to stare at fat people, short people, burn victims, anorexics, cripples— all those who as Joel-Peter Witkin says, "[bear] the wounds of Christ."

Even though we haven't paid for the right, we look anyway, don't we?

I suppose that nowhere is this fascination and flirtation with the grotesque more apparent than in art, particularly in film. I am thinking of Brueghel and Bosch. Of Lon Cheney's Quasimodo, Jean Marais' Beast, Bela Lugosi's Dracula, and, of course, Boris Karloff's monster as he appeared in James Whale's 1931 film, *Frankenstein*. There is no doubt that it was James Whale who made Frankenstein into the cultural icon it has become, even though he took a lot of liberty with Ms. Shelley's character. Or at least his screenplay writers did. It is little wonder, considering that the screenplay was written by four people based on a "composition" by John Balderston, which itself was an adaptation of a play by Peggy Webling. Several of the extraneous characters they introduced have since become in the public imagination an inextricable part of the story. Characters like Dr. Septimus Praetorius in the 1935 *The Bride of Frankenstein,* and Ygor, played by Bela Lugosi (who, interestingly enough, had originally turned down the role of the monster because he didn't think it was glamorous enough and because the part had no lines). Whale took other liberties as well. The laboratory which Herman Rosse designed for the film was a far cry from the "workshop of filthy creation" that Mary Shelley had young Victor Frankenstein living and working in at the University. Those rooms, according to Shelley, were equipped with nothing more than a few expendable lab fixtures that were given to him by his instructors, the Messers Waldman and Krempe, and a few surgical tools he probably filched from class. Shelley's character undertook his "midnight labours" in a laboratory that was a far cry from the fantastically appointed laboratory James Whale and Universal Pictures would have us think and Mel Brooks would have us remember so delightfully. Likewise, the filmmakers must have been uncomfortable with the name, education level, and youthful age of Ms. Shelley's "pale student of the unhallowed arts," because they changed his name to Henry, graduated him from the University, gave him a doctor's degree (maybe in Divinity, who knows?) and put a good fifteen years on him. But Mary Shelley's Victor Frankenstein was a very young man, a point that is crucial to the story. He was not at all the wizened and experienced scientist as the Colin Clive and Basil Rathbone film images suggest. No, Ms. Shelley's Herr Frankenstein was a sophomore at the University—a wise fool.

Nevertheless, the images designed for the 1931 film survive in the mind of the public as the kithless form of Mary Shelley's *Frankenstein*—with Boris Karloff as the only Monster. This despite the fact that the first Frankenstein monster appeared in film as early as in 1910 in a picture made by Thomas Edison and Edison Films. In that version, the monster was portrayed by Charles Ogle, a minister's son from Zanesville, Ohio. Ogle, as was true of most performers of the time, was responsible for his own make-up. And to my mind, his interpretation was truer to the novel than any so far, although if Robert De Niro had been a little bigger and a bit more eloquent in his speech, he could have given Ogle a run for his money.

It is curious to me that there have been so many versions of *Frankenstein* in film and so few illustrated editions of *Frankenstein*, and, with the exception of the film-inspired comic book versions like that of Tom Barling, the pictures have been more decorative that substantive, Lynn Ward's notwithstanding. When I began work on the illustrations for Pennyroyal Press edition of *Frankenstein; or The Modern Prometheus*, I knew only one thing for certain. They would owe nothing to the film except for whatever subconscious scrap might be scurrying about in my psyche.

The original design for the Pennyroyal *Frankenstein* was a large octavo. I was going to leave the signatures unopened and unsewn. The illustrations were going to be printed on a different paper and laid into the middle of each of the folded signatures. I gave up on this idea because it unjustly diminished the text and self-consciously emphasized the illustrations over the story, and because I worried about someone spilling the sheets out of the case and onto the floor.

The second design was a quarto, and with few modifications, it was the final design. I used the Poliphilus types set on a generous measure and used paragraph marks for paragraphs rather than returns and indentations. I did this trying to evoke a machine-like precision and regularity and then tempering that regularity with the dark, quirky warmth and irregularity of Poliphilus. We chose the 1818 edition of *Frankenstein*, and used a copy in the Rare Book Room at Smith College for textual reference. It was bound, in the convention of the time for fiction, in three volumes. The boards of the Smith copy are covered in blue paper, and I thought it would be interesting and appropriate to recall those blue boards by printing blue inserts to be collated and bound between the volumes. What to print on those inserts remained in question for some time. Since we knew that we would ultimately approach the University of California Press about publishing a trade edition, it was reasonable to assume that the inserts should carry some sort of scholarly apparatus, making the package more attractive to them or another academic publisher. With this in mind, I commissioned four scholars to contribute critical essays: Emily Sunstein wrote a biographical essay called "Sewing the Blatant Beast;" William St. Clair wrote about the relationship between Mary Wollstonecraft and her father William Godwin in an essay called "Her Father's Daughter;" Ruth Mortimer wrote an essay on the bibliographical history of *Frankenstein* called "*Frankenstein*: A Publishing History;" and Joyce Carol Oates wrote an essay, "Frankenstein's Fallen Angel," which deals with the Gothic, fabulist, allegorical, and philosophical aspects of the novel.

Ultimately I changed my mind about the blue inserts because they broke the cadence I was trying to create with the overall typography. The essays were grouped at the end as a collective afterword. The University of California Press did publish our *Frankenstein*, but they declined three of the essays, choosing to keep only the essay by Oates.

I was not much older than Victor when I read Mary Shelley's *Frankenstein* for the first time. I was about to graduate from the University of Chattanooga, I was engaged to be married, and I was taking my first tentative steps in freeing myself from my family's blind reverence for Senator Joseph McCarthy and the vicious snares of their racism, anti-Semitism, and religious bigotry. Deep boils were festering in Montgomery, Oxford, Selma, and Birmingham. The Cold War was entrenched in Europe. Vietnam and the Gulf of Tonkin would soon swallow the life of my dearest high-school friend, Parks McCall. The threat of nuclear war hung everywhere like a shroud of death and fear. Berlin. The Bay of Pigs. The Cuban missile crisis.

That specter found resonance in my reading of *Frankenstein*: a monster created which, once unleashed, cannot be controlled, and, out of control, annihilates its creator. An obvious metaphor, yes, but one that stayed with me for twenty years.

My original impulse was to illustrate *Frankenstein* using this as a parable or metaphor for this modern, atomic age. I saw it as a döppelganger in the terms that Joyce Carol Oates defines it: a "nightmare that is created deliberately by man's ingenuity and not a mere supernatural being or fairy-tale remnant." To that end I collected images of Fat Man and Little Boy, of Pershing missiles and ICBMs, of Oppenheimer and Teller and Fermi, of nuclear explosions. In her essay Oates says that "*Frankenstein* is the picture of a finite and flawed god at war with, and eventually overcome by, his creation. It is a parable for our time, an enduring prophecy, a remarkably acute diagnosis of the lethal nature of denial: denial of responsibility of one's actions, denial of the shadow-self locked within consciousness."

And yet while that metaphor is perfectly reasonable and valid, I abandoned it. I abandoned it because I concluded that such a treatment would date the book for all time to come. "Oh, yes," some reader in the next millennium might say, "this book was obviously done in the 1980s." Books should be timeless, or as nearly so as they can be, and nothing dates (and cheapens) a book so readily as obvious political commentary—something I flirted with all too closely in *Oz*.

So, I reread the novel and re-evaluated my options. While it is natural and unavoidable that an illustrator brings his own philosophies and prejudices—his own political and moral agenda—into his work, I held for a while that this was not the ideal, pure form of the art of illustration, believing instead that the illustrator should be a servant to the text. Now I see that both positions are true, and the art of illustration lies in a delicate balance between the two. If the personal hue and cry is too obvious, the whole is diminished. If there is no passionate conviction on the part of the illustrator, the potential art becomes mere decoration.

I came to understand that, for me, *Frankenstein* is more closely aligned to other moral transgressions of the twentieth century: the failure of compassion, the reticence to communicate, the inability to empathize, and the pervasive and malignant presence of racism and bigotry. This became clear to me when the demon, in the second volume, eighth chapter, tells Victor about saving a young girl from drowning. He had no sinister motives—he saved the girl's life. Her lover comes upon the scene, snatches the girl away from the demon, and runs away. The demon follows—he doesn't know why. The man, seeing the demon draw near "aimed a gun, which he carried, at [the demon's] body, and fired. [The demon] sunk to the ground, and [his] injurer, with increased swiftness, escaped into the wood." The demon's feelings of "kindness and gentleness" gave way to a "hellish rage." Inflamed by pain, he "vowed eternal hatred and vengeance to all mankind."

It is hard to imagine that Mary Shelley intended any such agenda when, on that cold and rainy night in 1816, she told the story for the first time in that now famous ghost-story competition with her husband and their friends at the Villa Diodati on the shores of Lake Geneva. It is interesting to note that the tale Byron's friend Dr. Polidori told that night emerged in the spring of 1819 as *The Vampyre*. It is also interesting to speculate on the other tales that were not completed or perhaps told and never written down.

According to Mary Shelley's account of the origin of her "ghost story," the image of Frankenstein and his demon came in an extraordinarily vivid waking dream. She said that she "could not sleep," nor could she be said "to think." Her imagination, "unbidden, possessed and guided [her], gifting the successive images that arose in [her] mind with a vividness far beyond the usual bound of reverie. [She] saw—with shut eyes, but acute mental vision—[she] saw the pale student of unhallowed arts kneeling beside the thing he had put together. [She] saw the hideous phantasm of a man stretched out, and then, on the working of some powerful engine, show signs of life, and stir with uneasy half-vital motion ... the student sleeps: but he is awakened; he opens his eyes: behold the horrid thing stands at his bedside, opening his curtains, and looking on him with yellow, watery, but speculative eyes."

I looked at *Frankenstein* for a long time before making up my mind to commit to a more tenuous infusion of my politics into the illustrations.

The cue came, as it often does, from the typography. The blackness and rigidity of the type block, the drum drum of the machine-like repetition, the absence of decorative color (except on the first title page) suggested that I do something different for the demon, something to set him apart. I decided to use color. Warm color as a sort of metaphor of my empathy for him. I did not feel the revulsion for him that Victor did. He was ugly. My God, how could he help but be, wrought as he was out of parts scavenged from gallows, funeral homes, and slaughterhouses? In fact his ugliness is, as Oates points out in her essay, the psychological center of the novel and, though I flirted with the idea briefly, I had no intention of making him handsome as some B-grade films had done. No, he was ugly and he probably smelled like rotten meat. It was the smell that ultimately captured my imagination.

I built a model of the monster's head using a plastic human skull that was lying around my studio as the armature. I fleshed out the large muscle groups with plasticene and removed some of the teeth. My daughter Ramona and I sewed together chicken skins that we removed from a couple of pounds of Frank Purdue's legs and thighs (at the time, I did not know that *perdu* in French means "lost"—a nice irony). We were careful to preserve the part of the flesh where, in an interesting and empirical demonstration of evolution, the feathers turn to scales near the foot. We sewed the individual skins together with coarse black thread using both surgical and upholstery needles. It was tough going and convinced me all the more that Victor's skills as a surgeon were probably not much better than ours. He wouldn't have done the job any more skillfully than we were doing it. We stretched the patchwork skin tight over the skull and sewed it up in the back so that it stayed in place. We cut slits at the eyes, exposing the ocular orbits, and inserted sections of ping pong balls with irises and pupils drawn on them. We sliced open the skin at the mandible and exposed the irregular teeth and the empty sockets of the missing ones. We didn't bother with lips.

I wigged the head with long black hair and fitted it out in a period hat. We set him out in the back yard on top of a tripod. I photographed him each day trying to catch the fall of different light and shadow and to document the process of decay.

Ultimately the summer sun rendered all the fat out of the skin and drew it even more tightly across the bones and plasticene. And of course the maggots came. Along with the smell. I memorized the writhing of the maggots and the smell of dead flesh and blended it in my mind with the words Victor uttered when he had finished sewing together his blatant beast: "How can I describe my emotions at this catastrophe, or how delineate the wretch whom, with such infinite pains and care, I had endeavored to form? ... I had worked hard for nearly two years, for the sole purpose of infusing life into an inanimate body. For this I had deprived myself of rest and health. I had desired it with an ardor that far exceeded moderation; but now that I had finished, the beauty of the dream vanished, and breathless horror and disgust filled my heart. Unable to endure the aspect of the being I had created, I rushed out of the room, and continued a long time traversing my bedchamber, unable to compose my mind to sleep." Victor does sleep but he is startled out of it. He says, "A cold dew covered my forehead, my teeth chattered, and every limb became convulsed; when, by the dim and yellow light of the moon, as it forced its way through the window shutters, I beheld the wretch, the miserable monster I had created. He held up the curtain of the bed; and his eyes, if eyes they may be called, were fixed on me. His jaws opened, and he muttered some inarticulate sounds, while a grin wrinkled his cheeks." Victor ran away, abandoning his comically monstrous eight-foot-tall baby and abdicating his responsibility. Ugly as he was, the monster was at this point free of all evil. He didn't become evil until he suffered the pain of denial and rejection. Denial and rejection based solely on the basis of his physical appearance. He could have been a Navajo in 1850, or a Japanese-American in 1942, or a Jew in Nazi Germany, or an African-American in Philadelphia, Mississippi in 1964. For this I gave him color. No one else. Just him.

I give a hint of his physiognomy in the first volume, a little sneak preview of sorts, a bit of the sutured hand beneath the surgical shroud—not that I believe Victor would have been so careful to use surgical dressings: the drapery made a more interesting image. But there is no color. The color comes in the second volume where it develops in a crescendo behind the sequence of black portraits of the demon, imitating the way light falls and modulates

from a fire in a fireplace, a fireplace like that of the cabin where the demon
sat Victor down to tell him his story. Conversational portraits I call them.
The eight illustrations are titled with words from the demon's own mouth:

"All men hate the wretched."
"Fire gives light as well as heat."
"Divine sounds enchanted me."
"My organs were indeed harsh."
"No father had watched my infant days."
"Hateful day when I relieved life."
"Cursed, cursed creator!"
"All joy was but a mockery!"

These are the bulk of the illustrations in the second volume. They are sand-
wiched between two panels of an Alpine diptych, the first panel of which
comes after an image of Victor sailing alone at night on Lake Geneva. This
sailing image is repeated in volume three, where it is set in the daytime and
Victor is sailing with his fiancee, Elizabeth. It is one of several double
images, designed as graphic döppelgängers.

The first of these double images is Victor's dream of Elizabeth, the dream
he is having during a fitful sleep when he is awakened by his demon grinning at him. He did sleep he says, but it was in vain: "I thought I saw Elizabeth," he says, "in the bloom of health, walking in the streets of Ingolstadt.
Delighted and surprised I embraced her; but as I imprinted the first kiss on
her lips, they became livid with the hue of death; her features appeared to
change, and I thought that I held the corpse of my dead mother in my arms;
a shroud enveloped her form, and I saw the grave-worms crawling in the
folds of the flannel. I startled from my sleep in horror." This scene, a composition of a figure (Elizabeth *cum* Victor's Mother) in shrouds, is repeated
later on when Victor is engaged in making the demon a mate in agreement
for the staying of his murderous occupations. The demon told Victor that
he was alone, and miserable, and that no one would associate with him;
but, "one as horrible as myself would not deny herself to me. My companion must be of the same species, and have the same defects. This being you

must create." Victor acquiesces to the demon's demands. Later on he reflects. "During my first experiment, a kind of enthusiastic frenzy had blinded me to to the horror of my employment; my mind was intently fixed on the sequel of my labor, and my eyes were shut to the to the horror of my proceedings. But now I went to it in cold blood, and my heart often sickened at the work of my hands." Victor has come a long way from his desire to "banish disease from the human frame, and render man invulnerable to all but a violent death."

All along the demon watches expectantly, marking Victor's progress.

Then "with a sensation of madness" and "trembling with passion," Victor "tore to pieces" the demon's unfinished mate. The demon saw the butchering and cried out, "I have endured incalculable fatigue, and cold, and hunger; do you dare destroy my hopes ... Shall each man find a wife for his bosom, and each beast have his mate, and I be alone? I had feelings of affection, they were requited by detestation and scorn ... I shall go; but remember, I shall be with you on your wedding-night." The double image seeks to draw an equation between the demon's bride and Elizabeth because although the sophomoric Victor thinks the demon is threatening him, the threat is directed toward Elizabeth, Victor's bride-to-be. *Quid pro quo.*

There are other double images as well. The demon's nascent hand is repeated in the hand of his might-have-been mate (plate 16). That the gesture of the fingers is reminiscent of the hand of Adam in Michelangelo's *The Last Judgment* is not coincidence. There is something of Adam in the demon—something other than not having had an umbilical cord—both were born innocent and without sin. Both were originally good. "Like Adam," the demon says, "I was created apparently united by no link to any other being in existence; but his state was far different from mine in every other respect. He had come forth from the hands of God a perfect creature, happy and prosperous, guarded by the especial care of his Creator; he was allowed to converse with, and acquire knowledge from beings of a superior nature: but I was wretched, helpless and alone."

The frontispieces of volume one and of volume two are truer mirror images of each other, recalling the demon's statement that he was but a "blasted stump," and mirroring it with Victor's belief that the "stream of fire" he saw issue from an old and beautiful oak outside his house in Belrive when he was about fifteen years old was the seminal moment in his creative life. Victor had never beheld anything so utterly destroyed. He said, "The catastrophe of this tree excited my extreme astonishment; and I eagerly inquired of my father the nature and origin of thunder and lightning." His father explained the principles of electricity, and Victor's life was altered forever. His, his family's, and his friends.

The final portrait is printed blue under black. Ice blue. It comes at the end of volume three, and occurs just before the demon flees across the arctic ice towards his presumed self-immolation. We are at the point in the story where the creature has exacted his justice and stands hulking above Victor Frankenstein, dead in his coffin. The scene is the interior of a ship. Everything is in motion. Language alone is a gyroscope. I paraphrase the demon's words as he says goodbye to his creator:

"Farewell, Victor. Your miserable corpse will be the last human thing these sorry eyes of mine will ever see. You wanted me dead because I killed your family, didn't you? But you denied me mine, remember, Victor? Remember the night you threw her lifeless body into the North Sea? But believe me, as miserable as you were, I have been worse. My pain is greater than yours. But death is coming to heal my wounds and I will no longer feel this pain. I will go now and walk into the torturing flames of my own death out there on the ice and I will take joy in the agony. And then, when the flames die down and the ashes grow cold and blow across the frozen sea, my soul will at last be at peace. So … farewell, Frankenstein. Farewell."

Five Self-Interviews

REGARDING JONAH AND THE WHALE

Friday June 13, 1997

I don't mean to be rude, Mr. Moser, but you know that if a man were inside a fish, or any vertebrate animal for that matter, it would be dark and you wouldn't be able to see. And even if it weren't dark you certainly wouldn't be able to see the ribs of the animal because you would be inside any one of a number a alimentary organs—and even if you could see the ribs they would be covered with sinew and muscle.   A: Oh give me a break. Q: But it's precisely the sort of thing you're always critical of. Even when you were a kid you saw this flaw in a very similar setting—in the Walt Disney version of *Pinocchio* when Gepetto is inside the whale. You thought even then that it wasn't a realistic interior. Remember?   A: Now that you bring it up, yes, I do remember. But let me correct you on one matter—I am not *always* critical of everything. And what the Disney people did was important enough to keep looking. Gill and I are interested in different things. He was more high-minded than I. He was making dignified images that appealed to, what shall I say, the liturgy of the church? I am making images born out of humanation that show all the warts, pimples, frailties, and scars of the human condition. I want somebody to look at my Daniel and think, "Jeez, he sure looks a lot like ol' Effren works down to Jiffy Lube." In other words, I am not interested in aristocratic, romanticized, generalized, or idealized Biblihabitants. In my mind's eye I am seeing the kind of people who handle serpents while they praise God. "The saints of God," as Sister Barb put it. Gill was interested in iconography, not narrative. His engraving technique and style lent itself to icons, particularly in the way they worked with letters, and I think he therefore gravitated toward that style naturally, perfected it, and sought, like we all do, to rationalize it. When he said that representational images were inappropriate to religious art he might well have been doing exactly what I am doing here.   Q: Which is what?   A: Answering my critics before they challenge me. But let me continue my argument—I made the choice to make statements, tell stories, and ask questions with my pictures and NOT to make icons or decorations. The statements, questions, and stories, if they are to be accessible to (forgive the seeming condescension) the common man, have to be in a vernacular that he does not have to confront, a vernacular that he can understand, accept, and get beyond. The common man rarely understands how images are made. Rarely understands the myriad considerations that go into them, and that's a problem for someone like me who wants so badly to communicate with him—Camus said something to that effect in *The Myth of Sisyphus*. I think Gill's iconographic style, while lovely to me and Bruce Kovner and Lenny Baskin, confronts the common man. Forces him to think about the image first and to postpone whatever else Gill intends the image to do till some time later on. I ask the common man to think about the image last. I want him to think about the story first. Or to meditate on the question I am asking. Or to consider the theological or historic position I might be taking. Illustration, at least narrative illustration, should be invisible (to borrow a typographic *bon mot* from Gill himself). Technique and style should never interfere with that process. It should never, as John Gardner says, awaken the reader from the fictive, or in this case, the Biblical dream. Now if I were doing this book for the intelligentsia alone, I might consider abstractions—after all I was schooled in that manner. Or I might consider images that are coolly ambiguous, obscure, and inscrutable. But I am not doing this book for that audience—though I trust that they will appreciate it as well, if for different reasons and on the various levels I am trying to build into it. No, my primary audience is the same as what I perceive Dürer's, Goya's, Camus', and Rembrandt's to have been: ordinary people who have little idea of what the art process, what (if you will forgive my using one of my most despised words) the creative process is about. It's like the Mass in a way. How many people who have heard—or hear—of one William Byrd's masses understand the architectural and tonal structure? Do you reckon that Byrd sought to appeal only to those who understood the complexities of counterpoint and the motet form to partake, by way of hearing the music, in the celebration of the Eucharist and the praising of God? I think not. Is that enough of an answer to your question? Q: It is for me.

REGARDING THE PROPHET EZEKIEL

Saturday July 11, 1997

Q: Regarding Ezekiel, Mr. Moser. You depict him as crazed (plate 17). Are you suggesting that the Bible was written by crazies? A: This is the only time—so far—that I have presented a demented character. I am not making a habit of it, but here I think it is appropriate: people of vision, especially prophetic vision, have been seen as crazy by their contemporaries—I think history bears me out on this. And it makes particularly good sense in the figure of Ezekiel. Think about it. The poor bastard was in exile. He was a recluse who was "afflicted with fits of dumbness and immobility." His prophecies were scorned by his contemporaries. He was forbidden to mourn for his wife when she died. He lived among briars and thorns and dwelled with scorpions. And he had to eat shit. Don't you think that things like that would drive a man mad? So, yes, I show a crazed man, but that does not necessarily extend to say, Isaiah or Peter. Maybe Paul (plate 18) a little bit. John on Patmos.   Q: What about that dog?   A: The dog was put there, to quote Whistler, because I "needed black at that spot." Beyond that purely formal reason, it becomes a kind of accidentally appended metaphor since dogs were not popular among Jews, and thus when a Jew called somebody a dog, it was an insult.   Q: Why not a cat?   A: You know as well as I do that the word cat is never mentioned in the Bible. You also know that I intend to put one in somewhere, just where I don't know yet, but wherever it is I hope it to be pertinent.

REGARDING SKETCHES

Thursday June 25, 1998

Q: I notice that when you begin to engrave the images you don't return to the file cabinet and retrieve the photographs, scrap, or sketches to work from. Why is that?   A: As you well know, I do sometimes consult the sketches. Not often though. When I do it's usually because I've drawn something awkwardly when transferring the image to the block and can't make sense out of what I've done. Otherwise, once I have the image on the block I tend to treat everything that has come before it, all the antecedents and all the sketches, as irrelevant to what I'm doing. At this point I'm onto the real thing—or at least onto developing the surface that will yield the real thing—and what I do on the block is all that matters.   Q: But you spend so much time refining the sketches. It seems strange that you would abandon all that.   A: I haven't abandoned it. The image of *The Leper*, for instance, will be very similar to the sketch no matter what I do. It doesn't make any difference if I look at the sketch or not.   Q: Did you look at the sketch as you were redrawing the image on the block?   A: You know I didn't. Listen, the point is that I don't want the sketches—no matter how finished they seem, no matter how much time and effort I have put into them—to dictate what the engraving is going to look like any more than I want the scrap I select and process into the finished image to dictate what that finished image is going to look like. Once I begin engraving, the engraving must take over for its own sake. It takes on a life of its own at this point, divorced from its beginnings. It owes nothing to anything that has come before.

REGARDING DIVINE INTERVENTION

Friday September 4, 1998

Q: You really do believe that God is intervening in this work, don't you, you old reprobate?   A: I wish I could believe that.   Q: Honestly now—deep down you do have a sense that something—even if you don't choose to call it God—is at work here. Something other than your own puny self. A: Yes.   Q: What is it then?   A: I don't know. It just seems that time after time when something like this Virgin image has to be done over again, or in this specific case *over and over*, I always come up with something that makes the whole of the work better—even if it has to be done over for reasons that are extra-pictorial.   Q: What do you mean by that?   A: You know. This image was redone because the second block I cut wasn't printing properly—and it was a redo of the first block because I mis-measured that block and cut it too short. If the second block had printed properly I would never have thought about doing it over again. But now that I have done it over again I can't imagine that I would have let either the first or the second version actually fly.   Q: Well why do you resist so strongly admitting that it might be God at work here? You used to believe that God was omnipotent, that He could do anything. You used to believe that He directed your life. That He kept you from danger—like that day in 1958 when you damned near got shot. That threw you into the ministry, albeit you were a boy. Now you resist the possibility of divine intervention.

Why?   A: Why do you call God "He?"   Q: Convention. I don't believe anymore than you do that God has any sex. But that's beside the point. You're avoiding my question.   A: I know I am. I don't know why I resist. I think that it is in part because it's too simple. To believe something like that is to deny the complexity of what God must be if God is.   Q: Why? A: Look at what Hubble telescope can see, for God's sake—damned near to the end of the universe, and at that it's only one direction it's looking in. It ain't even looking in *all* the possible directions. Can't, because there's an infinite number of them. Look at the structures out there. And that's just outer space. Same thing goes on in inner space. Huge, both ways. So huge I just can't imagine that any human being, pitiful and tiny as we are, has the ability to understand, to even grasp a feather of the wings, if you will, or a mote of dander from the hair of whatever created all that. This Bible is nothing compared to that. It's so insignificant it doesn't even count in the grand scheme of things.   Q: You don't know that. Besides, why couldn't an ability to appear simple to "pitiful and tiny" creatures be part of this unimaginable complexity you speak of?   A: I suppose it could be. Certainly it could be. "All things" the Book says, right?   Q: Right. Exactly. So, why don't you accept it? Embrace it. Maybe it would make you a more complete human being. A better person.   A: Because it's just too easy. And besides, I don't feel like there's anything spiritually broken and in need of repair.   Q: Are you sure?   A: Yes. Well...   Q: Oh, God, I give up. Why don't you just go get to work?   A: Hey, don't go bitching at me. You're the one with all the questions.

Moving in Darkness

Afterword to the University of Nebraska Edition of
Robert Louis Stevenson's
The Strange Case of Dr. Jekyll & Mr. Hyde

The illustrations for *The Strange Case of Dr. Jekyll & Mr. Hyde* were gleaned exclusively from Henry Jekyll's "confession" in the final chapter of the book. For me, relying upon this first-person narration made the images not only more reliable, but more personal and direct.

Placing them within the full text, however, was something of a problem. First, they needed to drum a regular cadence. Second, they needed to make sense within that cadence, and third, they needed to suggest at least a distant, though perhaps shadowy, logic.

My reading of the novella suggests that Edward Hyde is not merely Henry Jekyll's parasitic twin, as has been pointed out so often, but that he is also Jekyll's son, his "child of Hell" whom Jekyll midwifes in an "agony and birth" through a vehicle of a blood-colored "tincture" which boiled and smoked—in vitro, if you will. Jekyll himself says (in the third person, removed) that he had "more than a father's interest" in Hyde, and that Hyde had "more than a son's indifference."

I took this as a key and began the suite of twelve wood engravings with a paternal portrait—Jekyll's father (based on a portrait of Robert Louis Stevenson's father). That same portrait, ripped asunder by the black spite of the "wholly evil" Hyde, also closes the sequence. These two flanking portraits, the outer panels of a polyptych as it were, frame ten images which chronicle, expand, and suggest the dynamics of the "brute" son living within the father. To wit: Henry, a "schoolboy," walking with a man—perhaps his teacher, perhaps his father; Henry, a dark student beginning to assimilate the mechanisms of his tragic and ultimately fatal transmogrification (this portrait is based on John Singer Sargent's portrait of Stevenson, his head being supplanted in this instance by the illustrator's self-portrait, more or less); Henry Jekyll "laboring in the light of the day" in his laboratory (most definitely the illustrator's self-portrait); the physical transformation, seen only as comparative studies of two hands—one, Jekyll's, "large, firm, white and comely," the other, Hyde's, "corded, knuckley, of a dusky pallor and thickly shaded with a swart growth of hair" (plate 19)—a manifestation Jekyll observes in a "stupidity of wonder," "half shut on the bedclothes," bathed in yellow light (an interesting comparison to the yellow hue of Victor Frankenstein's demon); Hyde's "fancy," in which I mean to suggest "pure evil"—rape, murder, pedophilia; the "lamp-lit" streets where Hyde "gratified and stimulated" his "lust for evil" and where "terror" and "misgivings of the flesh" overcame passers-by who confronted the "inhuman," "ape-like" Hyde; Hyde's signature, which by slanting the cant of the letters backwards, Jekyll not only disguised his own "hand," but in fact created a mirror image of his own name (I wonder if in fact the name "Hyde" did not come about by Stevenson's writing the name "Jekyll" backwards in a mirror—so much he makes of mirrors); and finally I offer an enigmatic and shadowy image of Edward Hyde.

For this image I had originally intended to follow through with the self-portrait motif—the artist as Hyde—and went so far as to have my dentist fit me out with a carefully sculpted prosthesis of evil-looking teeth. But in the final moments I had to abandon the idea as being inappropriate. It was more important to stay in keeping with the text and, like Stevenson, not show Hyde's face. Easy and exciting as it is for me to create sensational and grotesque pictures, I chose finally to show the reader only that Hyde carries a heavy cane, that he is "deformed and decayed," and that he moves in darkness.

GOOD WILL & DISCRETION

A Note on Illustrating PILGRIM'S PROGRESS

ILLUSTRATIONS CAN DO a great disservice to a reader by fixing images so firmly and specifically in the mind that the reader is deprived of the joy and, indeed, the right to see characters and scenes however his or her imagination dictates. An illustrator's vision is his own. My illustrations are personal visions that I offer to the reader. I neither intend nor wish them to be definitive. They are visualizations of my opinions and should work much like a critic's comments—if they abet understanding, if they open new and unexpected possibilities, if they enhance the experience of reading the text or expand the reader's perception of the story, fine. If not, the reader should try to ignore them and make up his own.

For my part, I intended that the illustrations for *Pilgrim's Progress* suggest things to the reader rather than define things for the reader. Sometimes

I got carried away and told all about the hinges on the Shining Gate and the warts on Appollyon's tongue, but I left it up to the reader to supply the architectural setting for those huge doors and to decide for herself what Appollyon's tail looks like. Similarly, I offered my vision of Mr. Worldly-Wiseman and Simple, but I left it up to the reader to supply the faces and costumes of Interpreter and Mr. Blindman.

Since this story is an allegory about all people who search for truth and goodness, I show all sorts of people. Some wear fancy collars and plumed hats. Some wear overalls and derbies. Some are white. Some are black. Some, like Knowledge, contradict racial types altogether. There are no rules of place in this story, no rules of time, and no dress codes. After all, it is a dream, and all manner of weird and wonderful things happen in dreams.

Also, Christian is never seen up close—not like Pagan or Giant Despair (plate 20). His face is always seen partially hidden by the bill of his cap, or is lost in shadow or distance, or is turned away from us altogether. Only once, when Charity gives him his broadsword, do we get a glimpse of his face. He is an ordinary person. He is Everyman.

And when the author allegorizes a virtue, like Goodwill and Discretion, I treat those characters with dignity. But when the author pokes fun and throws darts I joined the fun with caricatures and satire, like Ignorance, Lucre, and Diffidence.

While the reader might notice all the above, what he or she might not immediately recognize is that the sky above Emmanuel's river is the same as the sky behind Appollyon. Or that the color red runs conspicuously throughout the book, both in the illustrations and in the typography. Or that the portraits have plain backgrounds. Or that the type is set on a narrow measure and always ends dead on center. Or that the Giantess Diffidence has a thing for pink. Or that Christian's roll is sealed with the Greek letters that stand for "Christ" and for "the beginning and the end." All these things have reasons for being. Or do they? The readers must be the judge. It's their story now.

Through Thought on Thought

On Illustrating Dante

I USED TO KEEP three books of drawings to chronicle and celebrate special occasions in the lives of my three daughters. I still have them tucked away in the library. I called the books *Liber Occasiona* and kept them up to date on a regular basis. The drawings were simple things intended solely for the enjoyment of my children. They were direct, quick, and understated. And because they were for my kids, they were personal and unselfconscious. They were not intended for the public eye. Allen Mandelbaum saw these drawings during a visit to my Northampton studio in 1977. I was working with Paul Mariani on our first collaboration, a book of poems called *Timing Devices* that Mandelbaum was helping to underwrite. While Paul and I kibitzed about the design and illustration of his book, Allen browsed my bookshelves. He came across the three *Liber Occasiona* and asked what they were. After I explained, he sat down in an easy chair, lit a cigarette, and studied the drawings carefully and thoughtfully. When Paul and I finished our work, we left the studio with Allen and his friend Laurie Magnus to go have some lunch. We were walking down the street when Allen asked me if I would be willing to do some "graphic meditations" (as he called them) to accompany his forthcoming translation of *Inferno*. He wanted drawings, he said, very much along the lines of what he saw in my girls' books of occasions.

I was taken aback by his suggestion. Taken aback and frightened by the prospect because I had never read Dante. I had heard of his work and had eaten a few times at a steak house in West Springfield, Massachusetts, that was called Dante's Inferno. Other than that, my only contact with *Inferno* was a perfunctory familiarity with some *Inferno* imagery, notably that of Sandro Botticelli, William Blake, Leonard Baskin, and Rico Lebrun. And it was not comforting to think of myself in that company. In fact, it made me self-conscious and uneasy in my gut just thinking about it. But the idea of confronting such a great and mysterious text—regardless of my nescience, the risks of failure, and the embarrassment of unfavorable comparisons— was just too delicious to pass up. And besides that, Mandelbaum wanted me to do them. It was his idea for me to come on board, not mine, and that in itself gave me confidence that otherwise I would never have had. He wanted the kinds of drawings that I could cast off the brush and pen with aplomb.

Six months later, I began the *Inferno* drawings. I worked on them for over a year, but most of those that appear in the University of California Press *Inferno* were, in fact, done during a single violently productive month— July, 1979.

In the two months preceding that ebullient July, I attended to the typical sort of chores that precede any illustrating job—drawing up lists of subjects, arranging the sequence of possible illustrations, and doing a lot of thinking and reading. I conferred and corresponded with Mandelbaum regularly, to the point of making a pest of myself, compiling ideas with him that were sometimes traditional, sometimes obscure, and (according to Mandelbaum) sometimes entirely new to *Inferno* iconography.

From the beginning I set two limitations on the drawings. First, they had to be tied specifically to the text, even if that tie were ambiguous. And second, they had to work within the typographic format that I had designed, working hand in hand with Mandelbaum (who had run a printing shop in Italy years before and was no amateur typographer) and with Chet Grycz at the University of California Press in Berkeley. The format, a facing page, line-for-line translation didn't allow for images being placed in the text itself. I suppose it could have been done, but the easiest and most logical way to address the situation, it seemed to all of us involved, was to do full-page images and place them, face to face, between every other Canto.

I think it is fair to say that most contemporary artists find such restricted formats too confining for their tastes and disciplines, and this is why so many have forsaken the canvas, or the wall, in favor of more "freedom." But I find restricted formats stimulating and challenging, I assume it comes from my love of typography and my love of the page. The fact is that the self-imposed limitations were an integral part of an attempt to break away from what I perceived at that time (and still do, to a degree) as a craftless and undisciplined obscurity of imagery, which—to my eye—had become fashionable and expected.

So I restricted myself, or more accurately, the form of the book restricted me. Nevertheless, I hoped to produce images within those restrictions that would be fresh and spontaneous and would be capable of standing on their own, full of life. Images that would celebrate craft. Images that would form a whole only when married with text and type. Images that would be as "original" as anything in the contemporary repertoire, given that I thought then, as I do now, that there is no such thing as originality

Before I actually began the drawings, I studied the Stradanus, Doré, Botticelli, and Flaxman illustrations for *Inferno*. And I looked at a little Delacroix, too. But I avoided my twentieth-century predecessors as much as I could. The immediacy of their company was too uncomfortable—and too tempting.

When I finally did begin the drawings, I began with thumbnail sketches—simple contours and quick gestures, abstractions really, that merely suggested subject matter and composition. It didn't take long for me to realize that a lot of my ideas were going to require visual resources that I would not be able to cull from my own memory or imagination. I was going to need more stuff to build upon than what I carried around in my head. So I began collecting resource materials: photocopies of the Stradanus, Doré, Botticelli, and Flaxman images; scrap culled from magazines and newspapers—particularly agonized faces and gargoyles; a plaster cast of Dante himself; and some of my own photographs—mostly figures shot from hired models, but also of twisted trees, dark forests, and stony landscapes.

And of course, as it always happens, most of the early ideas were flawed because they had not been thought through well enough. They had no real sense of direction or form. They were just dull, plain and simple. And they were thrown into the garbage.

On the other hand, some ideas came quickly, unbeckoned, and developed fully and immediately right there on the drawing table. There weren't many of these, but there were a few. Images like The Dark Wood, Farinata in his sepulchre, and the demons Scarmiglione, and Barbariccia.

More such images might have come early on, but when I went to stock up on the paper I had used for the *Liber Occasiona* I discovered that it was no longer available. That paper was Hayle, an English handmade paper from the Barcham Green mills in Maidstone. They still made it, but, unfortunately for me, not sized as it had been in the older paper. The new makings of Hayle absorbed the washes rather than resisting them and the crisp integrity of the brush marks and pen lines were lost. It was like drawing on blotter paper. I was further frustrated by the discontinuation of an extra-dense India ink that I had come to depend on. The combination was a minor calamity. I searched and experimented with all sorts of papers—drawing papers, watercolor papers, printing papers. Eventually, I found a mould-made Fabriano that worked fairly well for the simple, elusive, and ephemeral style Mandelbaum had seen and admired and wanted for his Dante. I also found that if I let my inks stand open, they would become dense naturally. Simple things to be sure, but in retrospect, I see that it was a crucial juncture. That was the time of the birth of Cerberus, of Manto, of Bertran de Born (plate 21)—all seminal drawings for later figures and highly reminiscent of the *Liber Occasiona* drawings. When I finished Cerberus, I knew that

I had found a surface that would do what I wanted it to do with ink that could be made readily available.

And so the stage was fully set and the final drawings started.

The gesture of each composition was stated first with a graphite pencil, loosely blocking the arrangement and placement of forms and figures, much in the vein of the thumbnail sketches. Then, using large Japanese *fude* brushes, fully charged with clean, clear water, I dashed, danced, and darted the water upon the paper, making invisible gestures over the pencil lines. Then, into those invisible gestures I touched and mingled the thick, black ink. The black exploded into the wet gestures spontaneously and uncontrolled. Accidents, if you will. As often as not the accidents suggested nothing and the drawing developed no further. A lot of them went immediately into the trash can. But if the accident was happy—if it was pregnant with suggestion—I developed it a step further. Slowing down from almost frenetic movements of the hands and arms to more controlled and deliberate actions of hand and fingers, I worked back into it, adding more brush work, pen and ink lines, pencil and charcoal. I reduced the blacks by scraping away the surface of the paper with a sharp knife. This process of adding and subtracting, subtracting and adding continued until an image, abstract as often as not, emerged which I felt was interesting enough graphically and formally to develop into a more finished state. Typically, several of these potential images were produced for each illustration. I explored them simultaneously—sometimes there would be three, four, or five drawings on the board, and more on the floor. I pushed them until, one by one, they fell apart compositionally or until the rendering of subject matter became awkward or contrived. And before long there would be only two remaining. And then finally there would be only one. As often as not, the ultimate decision of which one of the final contenders to develop into a final state was visceral and intuitive rather than cerebral and calculated.

This approach, as Mandelbaum observed and pointed out, was particularly appropriate to the text. The drawings danced, he said, as the language danced; they were expedient as Dante was expedient; they were quick and terse; and they were rooted in both Eastern and Western tradition.

When the time came, in 1981, to prepare the illustrations for *Purgatorio*, the apprehensions I had when I began the *Inferno* suite had been, if not dispelled, at least quieted. The major problems of format, iconographic approach, and the style and technique of drawing had been solved, establishing as a *fait accompli* the format and technique for the remaining two volumes. Consequently, I began the *Purgatorio* suite with a sense of ease and even a bit of daring.

The long, quiet meditations on my readings of *Purgatorio* and my lively, sometimes challenging conversations with Mandelbaum brought me to see that passion and suffering would be the primary themes of my *Purgatorio* drawings. Concentrating on the human face and figure, which are for me the most expressive vehicles available, I hoped to portray passion and suffering in a drumming procession of Purgatory's inhabitants and evocations—Manfred and St. Stephen; Buonconte and Omberto; Haman and Aglauros. Hope, of course, was also a presence—renewed in the angelic apparitions and in the stellar cross that preludes *Purgatorio*. The theme of close confrontation established in *Inferno* (there are twenty-nine pairs of eyes looking directly at the viewer) was continued in the *Purgatorio* suite, but with a passive rather than threatening character.

One hundred and fifty-seven drawings for *Purgatorio* were begun. Thirty-four survived. Those thirty-four drawings were culled, cajoled, and completed from amorphic beginnings, loose sketches, abstract gestures, and quick tracings as were the *Inferno* drawings: quick, urgent slashes of pale or clear washes laid over penciled gestures; mingling into that wetness dark washes and dense inks; adding and subtracting, exploring many solutions simultaneously.

I did not always know where I was going and most of the drawings emerged only through the act of drawing, such as *Arachne*, *The Isle of Purgatory*, and *The Helmsman Angel*. Conversely, I approached a lot of images literally and deliberately—searching, by way of the act of drawing, for a preconceived idea: thus came *Beatrice*, *Dante with the Seven P's*, and *Virgil and Statius*.

The *Purgatorio* drawings were generally simpler than the *Inferno* drawings, both in subject and in composition. This was due in part to my growing confidence and sense of ease. But in larger measure it was due to the text's continual revelation to me—a manifestation that would come to a climax, naturally enough, with the *Paradiso* drawings that were two years down the road.

The *Purgatorio* drawings were not only simpler than the *Inferno* drawings, they were also darker—another step in the revelatory procession towards *Paradiso*, from the frightening, complex cacophony and pain of precise, minutely limned images towards the great and profound quiet of mystery.

I began the *Paradiso* drawings in December, 1983, and completed them in January, 1984. I began the *Purgatorio* drawings in June, 1981, completing them on August 4 that same summer. I produced the majority of the *Inferno* drawings, as I have said, in July, 1979. That all of these drawings were executed so rapidly and spontaneously is significant to me. Not only because it harked back to the drawings in the *Liber Occasiona*, but, as I noted earlier, it produced a sense of dance and a sense of expediency. And as Mandelbaum again pointed out, the drawings were, as Dante is, quick and laconic.

By the time I came to *Paradiso*, the fears and apprehensions I had confronted when I began each of the first two volumes of *The Divine Comedy* had all but disappeared. Whether this was a result of the confidence that the translator and publisher showed in me, or the favorable critical reception the first two volumes garnered, or the fact that I was not familiar with many illustrations for *Paradiso*, I don't know. What I do know is that I was able to begin that suite of drawings with a great deal more confidence than I had the others. The five years between *Inferno* and *Paradiso* had nourished my intellectual growth and my artistic maturity. It had broadened my understanding and shored up my self-assurance. And, not insignificantly, it had made me more willing to venture new ideas and to risk grander failure.

As the *Paradiso* drawings developed, it became obvious that the primary underpinning of my drawings, the scaffolding as it were, for *The Divine Comedy* had all along been spontaneity. That was what Mandelbaum had seen that day in my studio, and that was what I had been trying hard to replicate, despite the fact that by the time I arrived at *Paradiso* I was moving away from that particular style and technique of drawing.

The second part of the scaffold was less obvious and did not become apparent for a while. I was surprised when I noticed one day that my images were progressing from complexity to simplicity. The logical conclusion of this progression, it seemed to me as I studied on the matter, would have to be toward complete abstraction. Toward a reversing of the roles of black and white, because after all, Paradise must be the opposite of Hell.

And that suggested the third part of the scaffold, which was tonal progression. The drawings for *Inferno* were distinctly high key and the drawings for *Purgatorio* were in middle registers. It seemed to me the drawings for *Paradiso* would therefore have to be decidedly low-key. The transition would ride from a pale Hell to a dark Paradise—the opposite of what is expected. And I liked the idea—for two reasons.

First, the torment of the Holocaust has influenced the tonality of most if not all post-World War II illustrators of *Inferno* (I had been looking after all). That horror has been reflected in dark and brooding tones and, rightfully so. But, for me, I see the Zyklon B gas seeping through shower nozzles when the lights are on. I hear the incandescent screams of mothers. I see the blinding light and feel the horrific heat of the fires of furnaces whose gaping maws devoured the corpses of murdered Jews. It seems fitting to me, then, that lightness, not darkness, is the proper graphic response to the Holocaust in terms of Dante's *Inferno*. If that assumption be true, then darkness is right for *Paradiso*; the great and profound quiet of dark contrasting the frightening, complex cacophony and pain of light.

And second, Dante's Paradise is full of brilliant lights that punctuate darkness. He gives us images of spirit-flames, the sun, and the Celestial Rose. Graphically, light can be represented only by the whiteness of the paper, and then only when it is surrounded by darks. And so to these ends, I had to rethink my medium and my technique.

That led me to conclude that whereas the drawings for *Inferno* and *Purgatorio* were conceived of as positive drawings (the pen and brush make black lines that are reproduced as black lines: black always equaling black, white always equaling white), the *Paradiso* drawings would necessarily have to be conceived of as negative drawings.

However, for the sake of coherency and unity of the whole book, the *Paradiso* drawings would necessarily have to be executed in the same manner and medium as the *Inferno* and *Purgatorio*, using the same tools and the same paper. The drawings would have to be done again as invisible gestures of clear water, urgently dashed upon the paper, and mingled with thick black ink. Ideally they would be even more spontaneous than the drawings for either *Inferno* or *Purgatorio*. But how to make spontaneous pools and mingles with white into black without changing the medium? Without going to watercolor or gouache?

The answer lay in the process of printing the book. It lay in the photographic process of reproduction. When photographed, the images could be reversed. Black would become white, white would become black. And when the reversal of tonal values happened, the overall sense of abstraction that I was trying to evoke was actually heightened. Indeed, not only was the abstraction of these drawings provoking, it was also sufficient to the language of *Paradiso*, and correct for the content. *The Sun, The Never-Ending Light, The Celestial Rose, Through Thought on Thought*.

Abstraction, however, was not sufficient for everything. Indeed, in many of the images subject matter was mecessary and important. But the problem there was how to get positive images within the negatives. So, in collaboration with Chet Gryz at UC Press and the printers in Florida, we decided to try an experiment (an experiment which would be child's play with today's computers and applications). The idea was to make drawings and calligraphic emblems in pencil and then have the printers superimpose them, as positive drawings, on the negative images. Thus was born *The Pool of Light, Beatrice, The First Star, The Resurrection, The Evocation of Florence, The Saints, Jesus, Mary,* and *The Eye of the Eagle*. The only drawing in the *Paradiso* suite that was executed in the positive mode is the Crucifixion. As a result, it and the frontispiece portrait of Dante are the only drawings from the *Paradiso* suite that exist as they were reproduced.

And, as I look back at it now, I see that those three books of drawings, done up by a daddy to chronicle and celebrate special occasions in the lives of his three young daughters, led me, as it were, to Paradise. And, with Dante and Virgil, they led me to and through the *malebolge* of Hell and the mountain of Purgatory. Drawings that were done in innocence and play and for the love of my children led me to become confident in my intellect and my judgement as well as in my ability to draw. Led me unwittingly and without intention to one of the major vectors of my artistic life. Led me to see the stars for the first time. *"E quindi uscimmo a riveder le stelle."*

Tenakh & Testament

A Reprobate Tinkers with Holy Writ

I BEGAN WITH THE CRUCIFIXION. It was, for me, the most important and difficult image in the whole book and I wanted to get it done and out of the way. That way I would be able to put it up somewhere in the studio and study it for the next couple of years. Change my mind about it if I wanted. Or do it over again. I decided to follow a safe course and do it as a variation of the Crucifixion I did for *Paradiso* fourteen years earlier. Doing so seemed to me to be not so much an easy way out (which it admittedly was) as it was beginning from where I left off. As the Tuscan himself said, "*Però d'un atto uscir cose diverse.*" "Thus from one action issued differing things."

But in some small, nagging crevice inside, it bothered me that I was restating an old composition, though I didn't know exactly why. It's not that I haven't done that before. I have. Often. It was certainly a competent image, interestingly composed with overarching implications of mystery and agony. But something wasn't quite right, and I knew it—not about the image, but about my lack of involvement in it, and the detachment that this implied.

I engraved it anyway, put it (and my critical judgment) aside, and moved on to *The Raising of Lazarus*. But as I continued making my way through the Gospels I could not stop thinking that I had missed something important back there at my first confrontation with Golgotha. Then, at the University of Kansas in April, 1997, I gave a speech about the project—a work in progress. I showed slides of a number of the images that were finished: *The Death of John the Baptist, Ecce Homo* (plate 22), *Mary Magdalene, The Annunciation*. Then I projected a slide of the Crucifixion and read the verse from Matthew that captions it—the one that says there "were there two thieves crucified with him, one on the right hand, and another on the left. And they that passed by reviled him, wagging their heads." Hearing myself read that text as I looked at my very comfortable image—a hundred times magnified—convinced me that I had to go back. Go back to Golgotha and start over again. Get involved in it personally. At dirt level. At the level where blood and dirt mingle. Do something that was distinctly not comfortable. Not expected. To bring it to a common, human level, like Brueghel did. To see it as a mother and child on the way to market might have seen it—out of the corner of their eyes—just passing by, not wanting to have anything to do with it (plate 23). Perhaps they were repulsed by the blood and screams. Hid their eyes. Perhaps the child asked, "Why, mamma?" and the mother couldn't answer. And they moved on, needing to get by the black-browed, venomous crowd and go on with their lives. Go home and fix dinner. Tell a story. Go to sleep. Yet others didn't pass by. They stopped, stayed and watched. Perhaps talked politics. Or religion. Laughed at the men hanging from the three trees, bleeding. Flapped their arms, maybe, in imitation of the crows that pecked at the eyes and living flesh of Christ and the two thieves. Maybe a vendor sold snacks—popcorn and corn dogs, like at a football game. And then of course there were those that stayed because they loved the man—the men—and wanted to help them through the indigo darkness that was about to overcome the noon. Their mournful sobs overwhelmed by the din of sniggering laughter, sarcastic derisions, the squawking of carrion birds, and the growling of feral dogs bickering over the blood dripping from the feet, about to bite in and help expedite the inevitable death.

However, if one accepts the doctrine of the New Testament, one has to come to grips, it seems to me, with the fact that Jesus died for these people who laughed at him and reviled him as much as he did for those who mourned and ached in their hearts for him. The earlier, comfortable composition did not say that. To say what I needed to say I had to abandon and compromise the classic balance and rhythm I typically try to employ in my compositions. I had to introduce foreign elements: the currish, malicious crowd—eating and scorning with laughter; a dog in the right panel— symbol of Rome, and a more complicated, resonating symbol when one considers that one of the many causes of death for a crucified person was loss of blood from his having his lower legs torn open by scavenging dogs; and birds—the sounds of the birds, harbingers of death, who went first for the eyes and there wasn't anything the poor bastard could do about it hanging there. Nasty stuff this crucifying. And an image of it shouldn't be comfortable. To tell the story, the image would have to be strident, discordant, and rude. And within that rough and obstreperous frame, Jesus is alone. Abandoned. *"Eli, Eli, lema sabachthani...."*

And I had to look hard at this scene, harder than I had looked before. I had to go there and look at it for myself. I had to be there, as the old hymn asks, "when they nailed him to the tree."

The poet Gerard Manley Hopkins once said that what you look hard at looks back hard at you. My friend Paul Mariani, considering this meditation, observed that it is especially so with the Bible. "You cannot keep coming back to the Bible every waking day," he said, "without the Bible speaking to you in turn. Eventually that encounter will seep into your life, your soul, and your dreams." One such dream came to me on Monday, January 11, 1999. In it I was making a small-scale, three-dimensional image of the crucified

Christ, something along the lines that Marisol Escobar might have done in the 1960s. The base of the image was a Resingrave block, one of the full page blocks for the Bible. Attached to it was an arm made of lath. It was perhaps seven inches long and one-quarter inch thick and extended outward from the upper left corner of the block. The face of Christ was drawn on the top edge. He was looking up at me, or perhaps at God. The expression on his face was benign and neutral. His pierced arm and hand were drawn on the lath and I was trying to attach that lath arm to the block. A man was helping me. He stood to my right side with a small hammer. As I held the block he began nailing the lath to it with a small three-quarter inch nail. I was looking down at the top of the block as the nailer did his work—looking down into the face of Christ, the face I had drawn. I held the block as steady as I could so the nail could gain purchase in the resingrave surface, but with each blow of the hammer I was thrown back. The face on the edge of the block began to grimace and then screwed up with pain. It screamed, and then I screamed. Screamed with the pain of each blow of the hammer, which was now larger and heavier than before—a two pound sledge. The nailer's face had become sinister and he kept pounding for all he was worth, grinning. Kept pounding until the lath arm broke off and the single nail protruded from the jagged, broken edge of the break. I said, "Oops, you hit it too hard." He said, "I guess I did." His face was sweet and pleasant again. There was man on my left now, Willem Dafoe I think, who offered to help me put it back together again. I looked at him through a miniature window I was fitting into the bottom of the block and thanked him for the kindness of his offer. That was when I woke up. I looked at the clock. It was 3:33 am.

Another night I awoke with the name The Press of the Redeemed Human Heart running like a stuck record in my mind. I don't remember what it was I was dreaming about.

Another night a small black girl, ten years old perhaps, touches two electrical wires together setting off an enormous explosion. A distant church is blown to smithereens. I could not see the explosion but I felt the impact of it, and then saw the dark gray plume of smoke rise above the nearby building. And I knew it was a church. I don't know how, but I had somehow collaborated and conspired with the child in the planning of the explosion. Other young people were involved too, but I don't know how, or even who they were. I went to the site of the ruins despite my fear of being discovered as the architect of the destruction. My fear of being caught was palpable and I had to choke it back as I walked among the shards of stained glass, kicking at some and retrieving others. Then, at a precipice, I looked over a heavy banister and down into a hole like the one Alice fell down—into Wonderland. The walls of the hole were teetering with church furniture, hymn books, prayer books, Bibles, debris, and more stained glass. A piece would give way and fall only to be snagged by something further down. Then something else would give way. Then something else. I passed on. And woke up.

I frequently woke up in the middle of the night with strains of Monteverdi's *Vespers of the Blessed Virgin*, Handel's *Judas Maccabaeus*, or Bach's *Saint Matthew Passion* singing loudly in my head—note for note, chord for chord, word for word. And I wondered if it was just that I listened to the music so much it replayed while I slept. Or if it was that the muse was visiting regularly during those days. Or if it was that a spiritual miscreant like myself was experiencing a state of grace and the night music was God's gift to calm a feverish imagination.

I don't know. People who do know things like this scare the hell out of me. Hal Crowther quite rightly observed that the "most dangerous thing about That Old Time Religion may turn out to be its contempt for doubt. Strong inflexible beliefs can be a great help to an individual. But when too many people hold them in common, almost invariably they get to believing that everyone should hold them."

Wislawa Szymborska, in her acceptance speech for the 1996 Nobel Prize for Literature, said that "torturers, dictators, fanatics, and demagogues [know] whatever they know [and that] is enough for them once and for all. They don't want to find out about anything else, since it might diminish the force of their arguments. But any knowledge that doesn't lead to new questions quickly dies out.... That is why I value the little phrase 'I don't know' so highly. It's small, but it flies on mighty wings."

All I know is that I had to go to work every day, the daily work of four years to make the images for the Pennyroyal Caxton edition of The Holy

Bible. And that was not an easy thing to do, making images for the Bible. Images that are reverent and respectful without being pious and obsequious. Images that are provocative and cause the reader to ask questions and see characters and stories in a new light. It's a daunting prospect—not so much having to do with the enormity of scale, though certainly that too, as it has to do with engaging a sacred text—and, vis à vis the King James Bible, it has to do with engaging and confronting what George Steiner has called the greatest monument of the English language. Having engaged this text, one then has to grapple with images that befit such sanctity and monumentality and has to wrestle with all the indigenous devils and angels that dwell within it. Moreover, one has to struggle with one's own arrogance. What light can anyone possibly bring to it today that Jerome, Aquinas, & Luther, Rembrandt, Caravaggio, & Chagall have not already brought to it? Beyond that, one must be up to the physical and intellectual rigors and must be willing to risk and endure the inevitable failures and criticisms.

And I don't understand. Why me? I heard no voices telling me that I had to do this thing. No publisher asked me to do it. Yet I was compelled to do it—and, in the quiet chinks of dark silent nights, it was a frightening place to be. Because that is where my fear manifested itself. If it had not been for the earthy snores of my big dogs and for the reassuring conversations I had in my dreams' imagination with the Virgin, and with St. Paul, I might have awakened and run away from it. Abdicated. Abandoned it. But I didn't, because in the daylight it was less frightening, but frightening nevertheless because such an undertaking assumes standards that go beyond the concrete and palpable nature of fine typography, good draftsmanship, solid design, and virtuoso engraving. Frightening because it is a polemical judication that assumes standards that are, by their very nature, speculative and extend toward the expression of opinions about God and the nature of divine teachings and Holy Writ. Whether or not I wished it or intended it, every time I made an image I took a theological position and this left me vulnerable to misunderstanding, miscalculation, naïveté, and stupidity. And in this I was alone. Despite the busy company of friends and family, I was alone. Despite all the love and fidelities and loyalties that embraces, I was alone with my work. And, perhaps, with God. I frequently wondered if I should have taken it on. Not about having taken on the work and the labor, which I love and look forward to every day, but about having taken on the cup of the unknown. The cup that is filled with that which compelled me to do this work. Filled with that unknown which I am so afraid to admit to. So afraid to call God.

And all this changed me.

All my work is transformative. Always has been. That's what work does when the work emanates from the mind. From the heart. But how it changed my inner life—my spiritual life, if you like—is an altogether different issue. On the surface there is very little change. I am still as much of a reprobate as I have ever been—a man who, as Benjamin Franklin said, can fart proudly. Can cuss. Can belch. And can spit natural juices and watermelon seeds with the best of them. I can be, and am from time to time, as sacrilegious, as bawdy, and as profane, perhaps, as those miscreants I placed at the foot of the cross. In many superficial ways I am no better than they. Underneath, though, this work brought me back to a familiar old struggle, one I had given up. A struggle with God, I suppose you would call it. Or with the idea of God. My struggle with the dichotomy of profanity and beauty. It has certainly made me less reticent to mention God in my conversations. I am Peter Schaffer's flawed Amadeus when he said to Joseph II, "Your Grace, It is true what *capellmeister* says. I am a profane man, but I assure you, sire, my work is not."

This work has even brought me back to prayer—and I don't mean clasping my hands together and getting down on my knees and mumbling Our Fathers. I mean the understanding that whatever God is, He-She-It knows my heart's mind and my heart's voice. I will never know what God is. I, like Aquinas, believe that whatever I can think God is could not be what God is—simply because I've thought it. For me, God is—and must be—a mystery. This work I have done is a song to whatever God is. It is an expression of gratitude for having the strength, ability, and energy to do the work and for the opportunity to live long enough to see it fulfilled. If that is not a state of Grace, I cannot imagine what is. And I cannot say these things about anything else I've ever done.

Now as I pass by this huge marker nearer the end of my life's journey than the beginning, I realize that I have been trying to sing my song to God all my life.

When I was a little boy and went to church with my grandmother I memorized the words of The Old Hundredth, and sang it gleefully—if not in tune. I apparently never could sing in tune. When I was in the eighth grade I was an enthusiastic member of the Junior Glee Club at Baylor, the military school I attended in Chattanooga. We were rehearsing *O, Holy Night* to present at the school's 1953 Christmas program. We were singing "For yonder breaks a new and glorious morn" when our young treble voices raised to sing "Fall on your knees." At that point I raised my voice as loud as I could. The sounds came from my heart: a pure, sweet sound in perfect pitch. And I was full of joy and pride in that transcendent moment. But then the coach—a tall, pretty, young woman—tapped her baton on the music stand and called everything to a halt. She stood with her hand on her chin, tapping that baton rhythmically on the stand. Then, looking directly at me she said, "Moser? Son, you just move your mouth. Don't make any sounds." I was crushed. Devastated. And, sadly, I've never sung since. Even when I was preaching, seven years later, I just hummed along with the music, sometimes trying to sing the words, but I never belted out a hymn no matter how full of praise my heart was. I was afraid of ugly sounds. Of praising God with dissonant songs. I talked about this with other preachers and they told me I ought to forget all that. They told me that God loves all the songs that are raised to Him—in key or not. But I cared. And I still do. With Flannery O'Connor I believe that God and posterity are only served by well-made objects. The only time I sing now is the rare moment alone in the car, gamely (or lamely) trying to keep up with Leontyne Price or José Carreras. But even though I don't sing with the voice of my throat I do sing with the collective voices of my mind, eye, heart, gut, and hand—the voices given me by whatever gives those things, whatever compelled me to do this work. And I daresay, in my effort to give something back, I won't be told to move my mouth and make no sound.

LABORS LARGE & SMALL

A Gallery of Engravings

I see only what is outside and what sticks out a mile, such things as the sun that nobody has to uncover or be bright to see. When I first started to write, I was much more worried over not being subtle but it don't worry me any more.
—*Flannery O'Connor*

FOR ME very little difference exists between making illustrations and making easel paintings or sculptures. Or for that matter between making visual images and verbal images. The art of making essays, fiction, and poetry is, to me, remarkably like the art of making pictures. It is so because fiction, poetry, painting, and illustration are all products of design, composition, and the tensions that exist between opposites. By that I mean the unexpected twists and turns that come about from the playing back and forth between the specific & the universal, the vertical & horizontal, the innovative & the traditional, the large & the small, the light & the dark, the simple & the complex, the abutment & the intersection, the comedic & the tragic, the expected & the unexpected, the trite & the profound.   ❦ It should be noted that the engravings included in this repertory were originally done to serve fiction or poetry and were thus seen within the pages of books inseparable from the text they served.

Plate 1. *And Moses Hewed Two Tables of Stone Like unto the First.* 1999. Relief
engraving (resingrave). 7.25 × 11.5 inches. From the Pennyroyal Caxton
edition of *The Holy Bible* (trade edition from Viking Studio).
Leonard Baskin was the model for this portrait of Moses.

Plate 2. *Icarus Agonistes* (state proof). 1970. Wood engraving. 9 × 12 inches.

PLATE 3. *Swinelike Bacchus* and *Goatlike Bacchus*. 1970. Wood engravings.
3.75 × 1.75 and 1.75 × 4 inches respectively. From *Bacchanalia*,
published by Pennyroyal Press.

PLATE 4. *Four Men of Printing*. 1975. Wood engravings. Each print is approximately 2.5 × 3.25 inches. Clockwise from the top left, William Morris, John Henry Nash, Frederic Goudy, and Emery Walker. From *Men of Printing*, published by Pennyroyal Press.

PLATE 5. *Moses in His Sepulchre*. 1999. Relief engraving. 7.25 × 11.5 inches.
From the Pennyroyal Caxton edition of *The Holy Bible*.

PLATE 6. *Jesus in His Tomb*. 1999. Relief engraving. 7.25 × 11.5 inches.
From the Pennyroyal Caxton edition of *The Holy Bible*.

PLATE 7. *The Great Whale.* 1979. Wood engraving. 6.5 × 10.5 inches. From *Moby-Dick, or The Whale* by Herman Melville, published by The Arion Press (trade edition from the University of California Press, 1980).

PLATE 8. *The Undertaker*. 1985. Wood engraving. 6 × 9 inches. From
Adventures of Huckleberry Finn by Mark Twain, published by
Pennyroyal Press in 1985 (trade edition by the
University of California Press, 1985).

PLATE 9. *Rosamond Naked*. 1987. Wood engraving. 3.5 × 6 inches. From
The Robber Bridegroom by Eudora Welty, published by Pennyroyal Press
(trade edition from Harcourt Brace Jovanovich, 1991).

PLATE 10. *The Beast*. 1992. Relief engraving. 5 × 7 inches. From *Beauty and the Beast* as retold by Nancy Willard, published by Harcourt Brace Jovanovich, 1992.

PLATE 11. *Alice in Her Sister's Reverie*. 1982. Wood engraving (detail). 11.5 × 16 inches.
From *Alice's Adventures in Wonderland* by Lewis Carroll (Charles Dodgson),
published by Pennyroyal Press (two subsequent trade editions
were published by the University of California Press, 1983
and Harcourt Brace Jovanovich, 1991).

PLATE 12. *Dorothy in the Golden Cap*. 1985. Wood engraving. 5 inches. From *The Wonderful Wizard of Oz* by L. Frank Baum, published by Pennyroyal Press (trade edition published by the University of California Press, 1986).

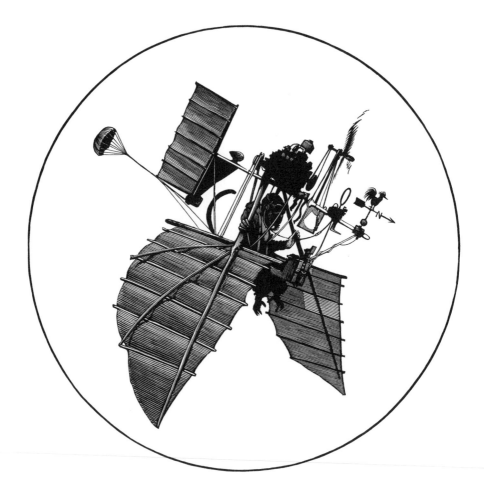

PLATE 13. *The Arrival of the King of the Winged Monkeys*. 1985. Wood engraving.
8.5 inches. From *The Wonderful Wizard of Oz* by L. Frank Baum.
published by Pennyroyal Press.

PLATE 14. *Sketch for The Wizard Unmasked*. 1985. Graphite drawing. 4.5 inches.

PLATE 15. *The Scarecow's Brains*. 1985. Wood engraving. 5.75 × 3.5 inches. From *The Wonderful Wizard of Oz* by L. Frank Baum, published by Pennyroyal Press.

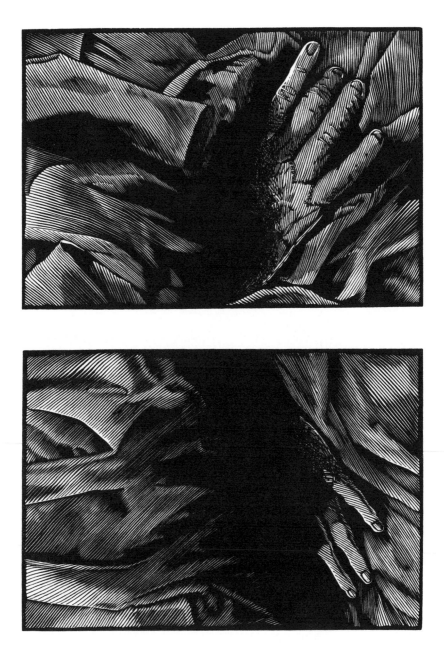

PLATE 16. *The Hand of Frankenstein's Demon* (ABOVE). *The Hand of the Demon's Mate* (BELOW) 1983. Wood engravings. Each 4 × 6 inches. From *Frankenstein; or The Modern Prometheus* by Mary Wollstonecraft Shelly, published by Pennyroyal Press (trade edition published by the University of California Press, 1983).

PLATE 17. *The Prophet Ezekiel*. 1999. Relief engraving. 7.25 × 11.5 inches.
From the Pennyroyal Caxton edition of *The Holy Bible*.

PLATE 18. *Paul in Prison*. 1999. Relief engraving. 7.25 × 11.5 inches.
From the Pennyroyal Caxton edition of *The Holy Bible*.

PLATE 19. *The Comely Hand of Dr. Henry Jekyll* (LEFT). *The Swarthy Hand of Edward Hyde* (RIGHT). 1990. Wood engravings. Each 2.25 × 4.25 inches. From *The Strange Case of Dr. Jekyll & Mr. Hyde* by Robert Louis Stevenson, published by the University of Nebraska Press, 1990.

PLATE 20. *The Giant Who Lives at the Top of the Beanstalk*. 1985. 6.5 × 9.5
inches. From *Giants and Ogres*, published by Time-Life Books, 1985.

THIS ENGRAVING was the basis of a watercolor image that illustrated Giant Despair in John Bunyan's *Pilgrim's Progress,* published by Wm. B. Eerdmans, 1994.

PLATE 21. *Bertran de Born*. 1983. Wood engraving. 3.75 × 8.5 inches. Based on the wash
drawing of Bertran de Born in *The Divine Comedy (Inferno,* XXVII: 118-126*)*
of Dante, translated by Allen Mandelbaum, published by
the University of California Press, 1980.

PLATE 22. *Behold the Man (Ecce Homo)*. 1999. Relief engraving. 7.25 × 11.5 inches.
From the Pennyroyal Caxton edition of *The Holy Bible*.

PLATE 23. *The Crucifixion*. 1999. Relief engraving. 7.25 × 11.5 inches.
From the Pennyroyal Caxton edition of *The Holy Bible*.

THIS IMAGE, one of two crucifixions in the Pennyroyal Caxton Bible,
is taken from Matthew 27:39: "And they that passed by reviled
him, and wagged their heads."

BIBLIOGRAPHY

Ahmadjian, Vernon. *The Flowering Plants of Massachusetts*. Illustrated by Barry Moser.
    Amherst: University of Massachusetts Press, Amherst, 1979.

Alighieri, Dante. *The Divine Comedy*. Translated by Allen Mandelbaum. Illustrated by Barry
    Moser. Berkeley, University of California Press, 1980–82.

Baum, L. Frank. *The Wonderful Wizard of Oz*. Illustrated by Barry Moser. Berkeley:
    University of California Press, 1985.

——, *The Emerald City of Oz*. New York: John R. Neill, 1910.

Barzun, Jacques. *The Use and Abuses of Art*. The A.W. Mellon Lectures in the Fine Arts, 1973.
    The National Gallery of Art, Washington, D.C. (Bollingen Series XXXV. 2) Prince-
    ton: Princeton University Press, 1974.

Beekman, E. M. *Narcissus*. Easthampton, MA: Pennyroyal Press, 1974.

——, *Carnal Lent*. Easthampton, MA: Pennyroyal Press, 1975.

Bell, Clive. *Art*. London: Chatto & Windus, 1914.

Blake, William. *Auguries of Innocence*. Illustrated by Leonard Baskin. New York: Grossmans
    Publishing, 1968.

Bronowski, Jacob. *The Ascent of Man*. Boston: Little Brown and Co., 1973.

Bunyan, John. *Pilgrim's Progress*. Retold by Gary Schmidt. Illustrated by Barry Moser. Grand
    Rapids: William B. Eerdman's Publishing Co., 1994.

Carroll, Lewis. *Alice's Adventures in Wonderland*. Illustrated by Barry Moser. Berkeley: Uni-
    versity of California Press, 1982.

——, *Through the Looking-glass and what Alice found there*. Illustrated by Barry Moser.
    Berkeley: University of California Press, 1982.

——, *Alice's Adventures Underground*. Facsimile of the original Lewis Carroll manuscript.
    Ann Arbor: University Microfilms, 1964.

Claiborne, Robert (foreword). *Word Mysteries & Histories from Quiche to Humble Pie*.
    by the Editors of *The American Heritage Dictionaries*. Illustrated by Barry Moser.
    New York: Houghton-Mifflin, 1986.

Crane, Hart. *The Letters of Hart Crane, 1916–1932*. Edited by Brom Weber. Berkeley:
    University of California Press, 1965.

Cocteau, Jean. *Beauty and the Beast: Diary of a Film*. Translated by Ronald Duncan. New
    York: Dover, 1972. Originally published in French as *La Belle et la Bête: Journal d'un
    film* by J. B. Janin, Paris, 1947.

Crichton, Michael. *Jasper Johns*. New York: Harry N. Abrams, Inc. with the Whitney
    Museum of American Art, 1977.

Crowther, Hal. "A Feast of Snakes." *The Oxford American*, No. 19, Oxford, Mississippi, 1997.

Cummings, E. E. *i, six non-lectures*. Cambridge: Harvard University Press, 1953.

Drimmer, Frederick. *Very Special People: The Struggles, Loves, and Triumphs of Human
    Oddities*. New York: Amjon Publishers, 1973.

Durant, John and Alice. *Pictorial History of the American Circus*. New York: A. S. Barnes and
    Co., 1957.

Faulkner, William. *William Faulkner at West Point*. Edited by Joseph Fant and Robert Ash-
    ley. New York: Random House, 1964.

Fox, Mem. *Dear Mem Fox, I Have Read All Your Books Even the Pathetic Ones: And Other
    Incidents in the Life of a Children's Book Author*. San Diego: Harcourt Brace
    Jovanovich, 1992.

Francis, Robert. *Collected Poems*. Amherst: University of Massachusetts Press, 1976.

Gardener, Martin. *The Annotated Alice: Alice's Adventures in Wonderland & Through the Looking-glass and what Alice found there*. New York: Clarkson N. Potter, 1960.

Gardner, John. *The Art of Fiction*. New York: Vintage Books, 1991.

Giants and Ogres. Alexandria: Time-Life Books, 1985.

Gill Eric. *An Essay on Typography*. Introduction by Christopher Skelton. Boston: David R. Godine, 1988. Originally published by Hague & Gill, Piggots, 1931.

Goines, David Lance. *A Constructed Roman Alphabet*. Boston: David R. Godine, 1988.

Gombrich, E.H. *The Story of Art*. London: Phaidon Press, 1950.

Graham, Douglas. *Bacchanalia*. Easthampton, MA: Pennyroyal Press, 1970.

Goudy, Frederic W. *The Alphabet*. New York: Michael Kinnerley, 1922.

Green, Ely. *Ely: Too Black Too White*. Edited by Arthur Ben Chitty. Illustrated by Barry Moser. Amherst: University of Massachusetts Press, 1970.

Hamilton, Virginia. *The All Jahdu Storybook*. Illustrated by Barry Moser. San Diego: Harcourt Brace Jovanovich, 1992.

Handel, Georg Frederic. *Messiah: The Wordbook for the Oratorio*. Forward by Christopher Hogwood. Illustrated by Barry Moser. New York: Harper Collins, 1992.

Hearn, Michael Patrick. *The Annotated Oz*. New York: Clarkson N. Potter, 1973.

Harris, Joel Chandler. *Jump! The Adventures of Br'er Rabbit*. Retold by Van Dyke Parks. Illustrated by Barry Moser. San Diego: Harcourt Brace Jovanovich, 1986.

Hill, Edward. *The Language of Drawing*. Englewood Cliffs, NJ: Prentice-Hall, 1966.

The Holy Bible. Illustrated by Barry Moser. New York: Viking Studio, 1999.

Homer. *The Odyssey*. Translated by T. E. Shaw. Illustrated by Barry Moser. New York: Limited Editions Club, 1980.

Hopkins, Gerard Manley. *The Journals and Papers of Gerard Manley Hopkins*. Edited by Humphrey House (Completed by Graham Story). Oxford: Oxford University Press, 1966.

Jacob, Dorothy. *A Witch's Guide to Gardening*. New York: Taplinger Publishing Co., Inc., 1965.

Maclean, Norman. *A River Runs Through It*. Illustrated by Barry Moser. Chicago: University of Chicago Press, 1989.

Mandelbaum, Allen. *Chelmaxioms*. Illustrated by Barry Moser. Boston: David R. Godine, 1977.

Mariani, Paul. *Timing Devices*. Illustrated by Barry Moser. Boston: David R. Godine, 1977.

Melville, Herman. *Moby-Dick, or The Whale*. Illustrated by Barry Moser. Berkeley: University of California Press, 1983.

Morris, Willie. *A Prayer for the Opening of Little League Season*. Illustrated by Barry Moser. San Diego: Harcourt Brace, 1995.

Moser, George. *A Family Letter*. West Hatfield, MA: Pennyroyal Press, 1980.

Moser, Barry. *The Death of the Narcissus*. Easthampton, MA: Pennyroyal Press, 1970.

——, *The Tinderbox*. Boston: Little, Brown and Co., 1990.

——, *Polly Vaughn*. Boston: Little, Brown and Co., 1992.

——, *Tucker Pfeffercorn*. Boston: Little, Brown and Co., 1994.

——, *Good and Perfect Gifts*. Boston: Little, Brown and Co., 1997.

Nelson John, ed. *Twelve American Writers*. Easthampton, MA: Pennyroyal Press, 1974.

O'Connor, Flannery. *The Habit of Being*. Edited by Sally Fitzgerald. New York: Farrar Straus Giroux, 1979.

Orgel, Doris. *Ariadne, Awake!* Illustrated by Barry Moser. New York: Viking, 1994.

Plath, Sylvia. *Above the Oxbow*. Illustrated by Barry Moser. Northampton, MA: Catawba Press, 1985.

Polidori, John William. *The Vampyre: A Tale*. London: Sherwood, Neely, and Jones, 1819.

Rylant, Cynthia. *Appalachia: The Voices of Sleeping Birds*. Illustrated by Barry Moser. San Diego: Harcourt Brace Jovanovich, 1991.

Shakespeare, William. *The Guild Shakespeare*. Illustrated by Barry Moser. New York: Doubleday Book & Music Clubs, 1989.

Shahn, Ben. *The Shape of Content*. Cambridge: Harvard University Press, 1957.

Shaw, George Bernard. *The Letters of George Bernard Shaw*. Edited by Dan Laurence. New York: Viking, 1988.

Shelley, Mary Wollstonecraft. *Frankenstein; or The Modern Prometheus*. Illustrated by Barry Moser. Berkeley: University of California Press, 1983.

——, Illustrated by Tom Barling. Grosset & Dunlap, 1976.

Steiner, George. *No Passion Spent*. London and Boston: Faber & Faber, 1996.

Stevenson, Robert Louis. *The Strange Case of Dr. Jekyll and Mr. Hyde*. Illustrated by Barry Moser. Lincoln: University of Nebraska Press, 1990.

Szymborska, Wislawa. *Poems New and Collected 1957–97*. San Diego: Harcourt Brace, 1998.

University Society. *Birds of Other Lands*. New York: Nature Lover's Library, 1917.

Smyth, Paul. *Thistles and Thorns*. Illustrated by Barry Moser. Omaha: Abattoir Editions, 1977.

Twain, Mark. *Adventures of Huckleberry Finn*. Illustrated by Barry Moser. Berkeley: University of California Press, 1985.

Virgil. *The Aeneid*. Translated by Allen Mandelbaum. Illustrated by Barry Moser. Berkeley: University of California Press, 1980.

Walsdorf, Jack, ed. *Men of Printing*. Easthampton, MA: Pennyroyal Press, 1976.

Wallis, Brian. *Andres Serrano: Body and Soul*. New York: Takarajima Books, 1995.

Welty, Eudora. *The Robber Bridegroom*. Illustrated by Barry Moser. San Diego: Harcourt Brace Jovanovich, San Diego, 1987.

——, *Place in Fiction*. New York: House of Books, Ltd., 1957.

Whistler, James A. M. *The Gentle Art of Making Enemies*. London: William Heinemann, Ltd., 1890.

——, *The Red Rag*. Easthampton, MA: Pennyroyal Press, 1970.

Witkin, Joel-Peter. *Joel-Peter Witkin*. Pasadena, CA: Twelvetrees Press, 1985.

Willard, Nancy. *Telling Time: Angels, Ancestors and Stories*. Illustrated by Barry Moser. San Diego: Harcourt, Brace and Company, 1993.

——, *The Ballad of Biddy Early*. Illustrated by Barry Moser. New York: Alfred A. Knopf, 1989.

——, *Beauty and the Beast*. Illustrated by Barry Moser. San Diego: Harcourt Brace Jovanovich, 1992.

Wolf, Leonard. *The Annotated Frankenstein*. New York: Clarkson N. Potter, 1977.

ACKNOWLEDGMENTS

Robert Francis' poem, "Poppycock" is reprinted by permission of the University of Massachusetts Press, Amherst, Massachusetts. The engraving of *The Great Whale* from *Moby-Dick: Or the Whale* is reproduced by permission of the Arion Press, San Francisco, California. Special thanks is due my editor, Jessica Renaud, whose wit and tireless energy managed to make me sound smarter than I am and shaped my words and sentences to sound more like me than they did in the early drafts.

COLOPHON

In the Face of Presumptions was designed by Barry Moser and Carl W. Scarbrough. The typeface is Galliard, a lively and lovely Renaissance face designed by Matthew Carter after the sixteenth-century models of Robert Granjon. Originally introduced by the Merganthaler Linotype Company in 1978, it was the first type of its kind made exclusively for phototypesetting. The italic is especially felicitous and just a little quirky, harking back to the models of the original chancery script from which the types of Claude Garamond departed. The hand lettering for the title page and the jacket is the work of Reassurance Wunder, an itinerant (and insolvent) letterer and slate roofer, last seen in Jackson, Mississippi. Mr. Moser provided two new relief engravings especially for this volume: *A Portrait of the Artist's Mother at Age Twenty*, which faces the first essay, and *Self-portrait at Age 59*, which serves as the frontispiece. The book has been printed and bound by Thomson-Shore, Inc., in Dexter, Michigan.